W9-CED-567

This edition produced in **1994**
for **Shooting Star Press Inc**
230 Fifth Avenue
Suite 1212
New York, NY 10001

© Aladdin Books 1994

ISBN 1-56924-071-X

All rights reserved

Created and produced by
Aladdin Books
28 Percy Street
London
W1P 9FF

Material originally
produced in the Rainy
Days series first published
in the United States by
Gloucester Press.

Printed in Belgium

Rainy Days

book of
PROJECTS

Written by
Vanessa Bailey and Denny Robson

Contents

Party hats	6
Costumes	10
Skeleton	12
Bumblebee	14
Placemats	16
Paper plate masks	18
Paper bag masks	22
Robot	26
Bright-eyed robot	28
Papier mâché masks	30
Papier mâché	32
Bits and pieces	34
Salad faces	36
Ginger cookies	38
Icing cookies	40
Peppermint creams	42
Marzipan treats	43
The educated egg	44
Eggs-periment!	45
Handy magic	46
The vanishing glass	48
Magic cord	50
Famous people	52
Pharaoh's finger	53
Levitation	54
Swordbox	56
Ribbon magic	58
Spot the dot	60
Suit-able trickery	62
Crafty glimpse	64
Burning building	66
Clever cut	68
Abracadabra	70
Dancing Dandy	72
Swinging monkey	74
Glove puppets	76
How to make Fiona Fairflax	78
Stick puppets	80
How to make the conductor	82
Marionettes	84
How to make the chicken	86
Hand shadows	88
Hand shadows with props	92
Making a theater	96
Simple puppets	98
Paper airplane	100
Balloon rocket	102
Parachute	104
Frisbee	106
Traditional kite	108
Kite flying	110
Clown kite	112
Flying the clown	114
"Instant" plants	116
Vegetable toppers	118
Jack-o-lantern	120
Miniature garden	122
Cactus garden	124
Warning, Clown kite	126
Handy hints	126
Index	127

Introduction

How many times, on a rainy day, have you felt bored with nothing to do? Or when planning a party with your friends, haven't you wanted to do something special but didn't know where to begin?

The Rainy Days book of Projects gives you all the answers. Packed with ideas to jazz up your party, entertain your friends or just create something out of nothing all by yourself, this book gives you all the inspiration (and instructions) you need to make fun use of your leisure time – using just bits and pieces of household materials that you can find around you at home.

So whether you enjoy making costumes, cooking, gardening, entertaining, magic, making puppets or models – just read on. There's something here for everyone – so what are you waiting for?

Party hats

Hats are always fun at parties. To make a very simple hat, cut a strip of tissue paper about 5 inches wide, long enough to fit around the head of the person who is going to wear it, plus a little over to overlap and glue. Fold it into wide pleats, cut out a triangle from the top and glue the ends together. Or you can make more exotic hats, just for fun or to go with a costume. They are guaranteed to make you feel special at your party.

You will need white and colored oak tag, tissue paper, cotton balls, paint, toothpicks, silver foil, thread, tape, glue.

Queen of Hearts
Measure your head with a piece of thread and use this when drawing the outline of the hat. (Remember to add a few inches so that you can glue the ends together.) Cover one side with pink tissue. Decorate with a braid of tissue along the bottom of the crown and tissue and cotton ball hearts at the top. Glue or staple the edges together.

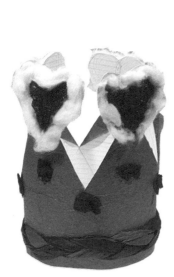

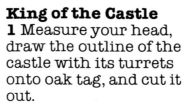

King of the Castle

1 Measure your head, draw the outline of the castle with its turrets onto oak tag, and cut it out.

2 Paint the castle walls. Instead of using a paint-brush, create an unusual effect by dabbing on the paint with a cotton ball.

3 Cut out a few flags. Attach them to the toothpicks with tape. Tape them to the turrets. Glue or staple the edges together.

Neptune's Crown

1 Cut a strip of oak tag to fit your head and cover it with silver foil. Draw the curve-shaped strip onto a piece of oak tag and cut it out. Cover with silver foil and glue it to the first strip as shown.

1

2

2 Cut out lots of little paper fish. Hang them from the top of the "waves," using thread and tape.

8

1

Woodland Crown

1 Measure your head and draw the basic outline of the crown, with its leaves, onto green oak tag. Cut it out. Cut out several thin paper leaves. Use green paper, or paint them different shades of green.

2

2 Glue the leaves to the oak tag, add a few strips of colored tissue for flowers, and glue or staple the edges together.

9

Costumes

Getting everyone to dress up can make a party exciting. Fancy costumes don't have to be difficult to make or expensive. Here are some ideas for you to try. Other favorites include pirates, gypsies, ghosts, and clowns.

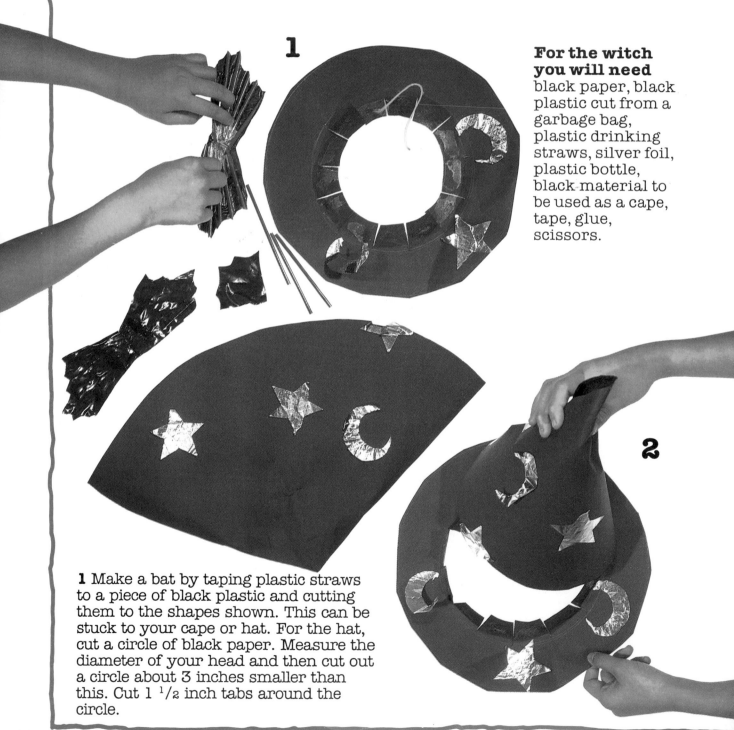

1

For the witch you will need black paper, black plastic cut from a garbage bag, plastic drinking straws, silver foil, plastic bottle, black material to be used as a cape, tape, glue, scissors.

2

1 Make a bat by taping plastic straws to a piece of black plastic and cutting them to the shapes shown. This can be stuck to your cape or hat. For the hat, cut a circle of black paper. Measure the diameter of your head and then cut out a circle about 3 inches smaller than this. Cut 1 1/2 inch tabs around the circle.

2 Cut a fan shape as shown to make the top of the hat. Decorate it with silver foil shapes. Roll it into a cone to fit the brim and glue its edges together. Fold up the tabs on the brim and glue them to the inside of the cone.

3

4

3 This creepy spider is simply the bottom cut from a plastic bottle, with eight long black paper legs.

4 Cover a book with black paper decorated with silver moons and stars for your spell book. Drape yourself with black material, add a few thread "cobwebs," a little face paint, and you're ready for Halloween!

Skeleton

This skeleton costume is quick, easy, and inexpensive to make, but it's very effective – especially at a dimly-lit Halloween party!

1 Look at the bones of the skeleton laid out on the page opposite. Copy the shapes onto white cardboard, making sure they will fit your body. Cut them out and use black paint or a marker to draw in the spaces between the bones.

You will need thin white cardboard or oak tag, black paint or felt-tip pens, scissors, double-sided sticky tape or safety pins.

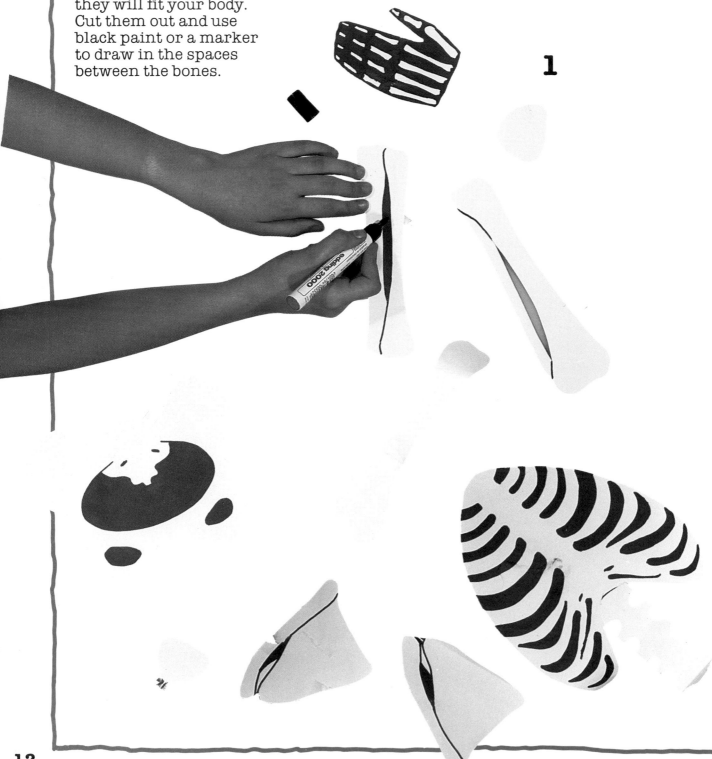

1

2

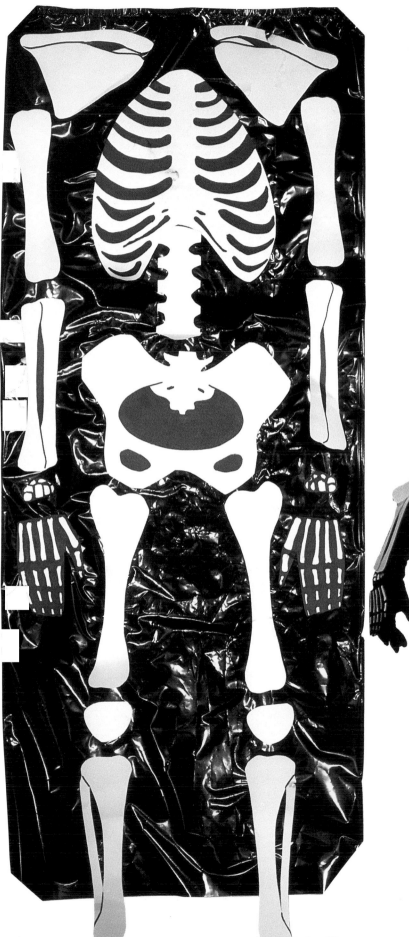

2 You will need to wear black clothes, gloves, and shoes for this costume. Lay out the bones in the correct order and then get a friend or adult to attach the bones to your body with double-sided sticky tape or safety pins. Use white and black face paint for your face and eyes to make the costume appear even more scary.

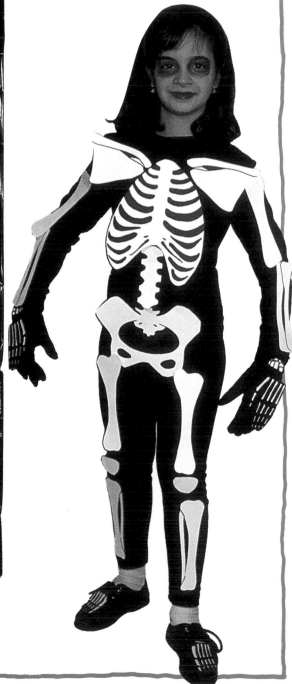

Bumblebee

This bumblebee costume would make a good costume for a younger child.

You will need a strip of black oak tag, two plastic drinking straws, silver foil, thin cardboard for wings, black plastic trash can liner, (or a yellow sweater if you have one), yellow cardboard or oak tag, pencil, felt-tip pens, scissors, double-sided sticky tape, safety pins.

1 Cut a strip of black oak tag to fit your head, and glue the edges together. Make two balls of silver foil. Make a hole in each with the point of a pencil and insert the drinking straws. Tape to the head band.

1

2

2 Cut out two pairs of wings. Decorate them as shown. If the paper is thin you may want to reinforce it by gluing another wing to the back of each.

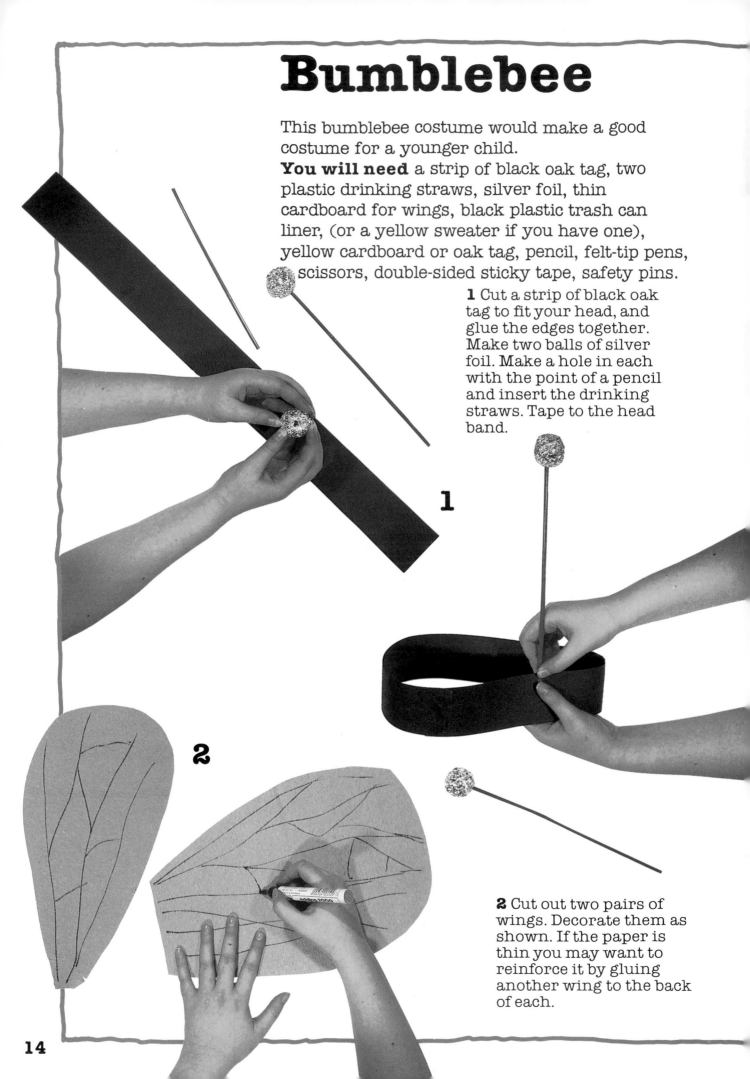

3 Cut neck and arm holes out of a black plastic trash can liner. Tear strips of yellow oak tag and tape them to the bin liner. Tape the wings to the other side.

3

4 Carefully put on the plastic liner and your antennae. If you have a yellow sweater, you could wear that instead. Pin the wings to the back and decorate the front with black stripes cut from a trash can liner.

4

Placemats

Make your party table look even more special with these colorful placemats. If the party has a theme, like the circus or an animal party, try to make the placemats fit in with it. If you are making faces, why not turn them into masks by making eyeholes and taping string or elastic to the sides. This could even be one of the party games. Get your guests to design their own placemat/mask and give a prize for the best one.

You will need thin cardboard, felt-tip pens, poster paints, a small sponge or cotton balls, scissors.

Draw your designs onto thin cardboard, making sure they are bigger than the plates you will use. Cut them out and color them in.

Or you could use stencils to make lots of placemats quite quickly. Design a face for the stencil, like this clown, or draw simple small shapes, like these balloons and presents. Carefully cut out the shapes. Put the stencil on top of the cardboard to be used as the placemat. Dip a sponge or cotton ball into poster paint and then dab it onto the stencil as shown.

17

Paper plate masks

Paper plates are a quick and easy way of making masks that cover your whole face. They can either be tied to your head with elastic, as with the party masks, or you can glue a stick to the back and hold them in front of your face. Experiment with different designs. You can decorate them with scrap materials, such as wool, dried pasta shapes, sequins, and beads, as well as with paint.

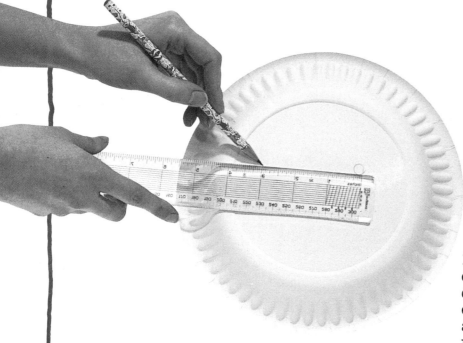

1

What you need
Paper plates, elastic or sticks, tape, glue, paints, tissue paper, string, an egg carton, and scissors.

1 Look in a mirror and carefully measure the distance between your eyes. Mark these points about halfway down the paper plate.

2

2 Make the eye holes by pushing a pencil through the marked points.

3 Attach elastic to fit your head, as before.

3

4 Paint the face. It could be happy, sad, funny, or fierce, depending on how you feel.

4

Paper plate masks

Sunflower
This pretty mask looks very effective, but it's not difficult to make. First, paint the plate a cheery yellow. Make the eye holes and outline with green. Cut "petals" from yellow and orange tissue paper and then glue them to each side of the plate so that they overlap. Finally, give the flower a smile.

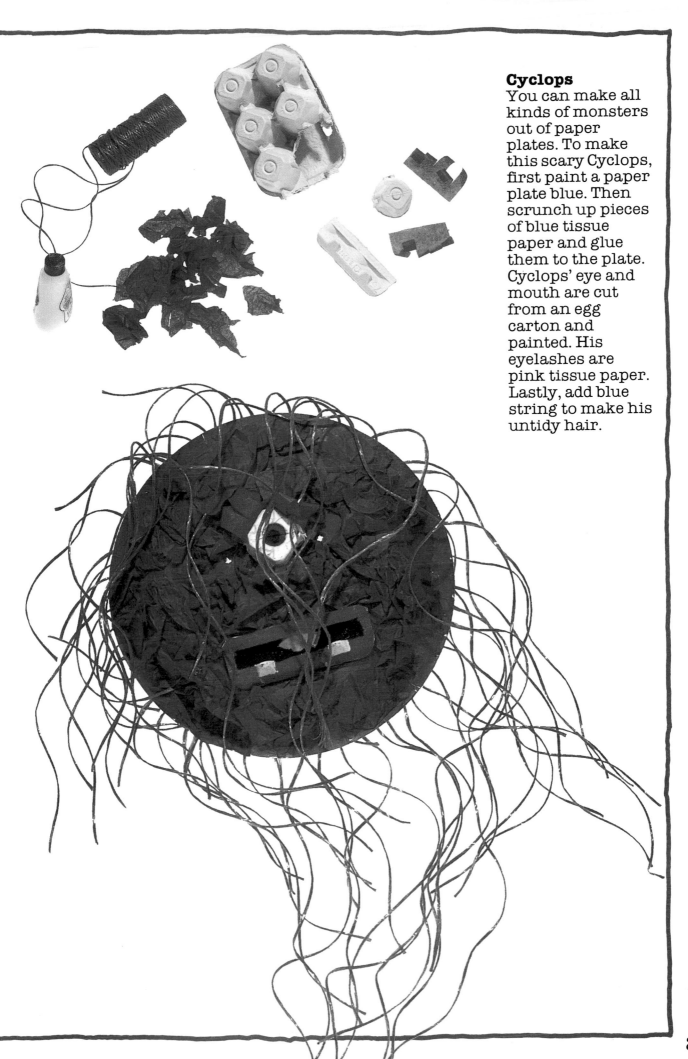

Cyclops

You can make all kinds of monsters out of paper plates. To make this scary Cyclops, first paint a paper plate blue. Then scrunch up pieces of blue tissue paper and glue them to the plate. Cyclops' eye and mouth are cut from an egg carton and painted. His eyelashes are pink tissue paper. Lastly, add blue string to make his untidy hair.

Paper bag masks

Paper bags are an excellent way to make really effective masks and headdresses. It doesn't matter if the bag is plain or printed. Poster paints should cover over any pattern. Just make sure that the bag fits your head before you start.

WARNING: Do not use plastic bags as they are extremely dangerous.

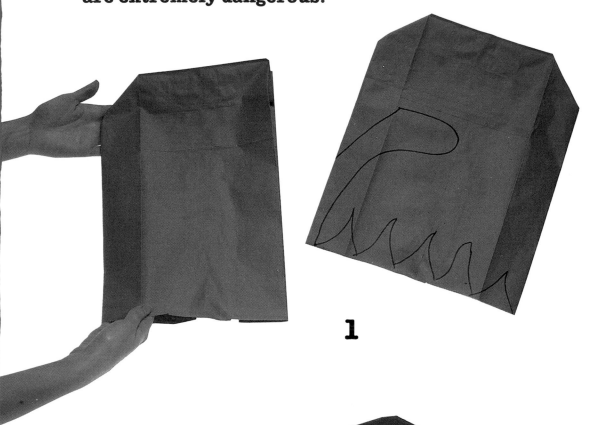

1

Eagle

What you need
Paper bag with a base, scissors, paints, and a paintbrush.

1 Flatten the bag with the base tucked inside. Draw the outline.

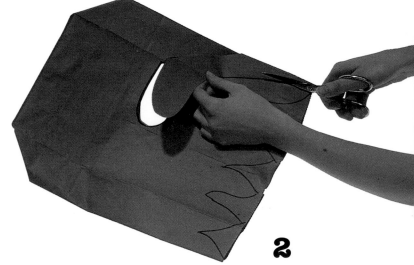

2

2 Cut between the beak and feathers, as shown.

3 Outline the features in black and then color in with bright paints.

3

4 Wait until the paint is dry and then cut out the feathers at the base. Wear the headdress with the feathers open, or clip them together under your chin.

4

Paper bag masks

The rooster

The rooster mask is made in the same way as the eagle. Again, the base of the bag provides the beak.

What you need

Paper bag with a base, orange cardboard, glue, scissors, paints and a paintbrush.

1

1 Draw the outline and cut out between the beak and feathers. Cut shapes from orange cardboard, as shown.

2

2 Glue the rooster's comb to the inside of the folded base and glue the other shapes to the sides. Finally, paint the rooster, outlining the eyes and beak.

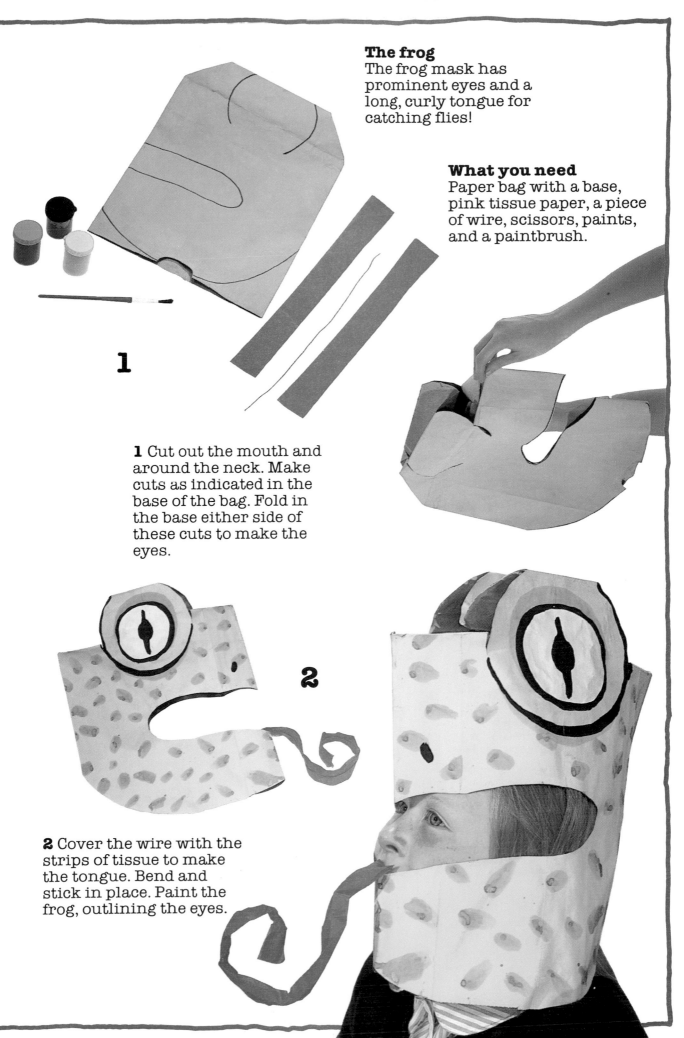

The frog
The frog mask has prominent eyes and a long, curly tongue for catching flies!

What you need
Paper bag with a base, pink tissue paper, a piece of wire, scissors, paints, and a paintbrush.

1

1 Cut out the mouth and around the neck. Make cuts as indicated in the base of the bag. Fold in the base either side of these cuts to make the eyes.

2

2 Cover the wire with the strips of tissue to make the tongue. Bend and stick in place. Paint the frog, outlining the eyes.

Robot

Three-dimensional masks that fit over your head can be very exciting. This robot is made from a very large cardboard box. It has armholes so that it fits over your head and shoulders, but a box that covers just your head would also work well. To make this robot even more spectacular, find out on page 28 how to give him eyes that light up.

What you need
Cardboard box, paper plates, toilet paper roll, small oblong box, aluminum foil, tape, and a piece of wire.

1

1 If the box is very large, cut armholes in the sides as shown.

2 Cover with aluminum foil, securing it with tape at the edges.

2

3 Cut the eyes and nose from a toilet paper roll. Use a small box for the mouth. Cover with aluminum foil. Make the ears from a paper plate, as shown. Tape all features to the box.

3

4

4 For the antenna, cover a paper plate with foil. Push one end of the wire through the plate and wind the rest of the wire around a strip of foil. Push through the top of the box.

Bright-eyed robot

What you need

One long piece of electrical wire (A), 2 pieces half this length (B,C), 1 short piece (D), 2 paper clips, 2 small light bulbs, 2 small batteries, and tape.

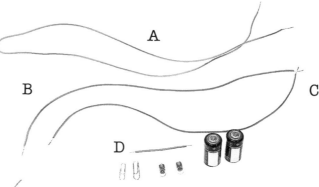

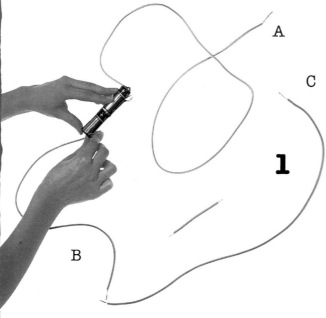

1 Tape the two batteries together, positive to negative. Tape wire A to one end of the batteries and wire B to the other.

2 Tape the batteries inside the box at the bottom. Make a small hole above each of the robot's eyes. Push wire A through one of the holes to the front.

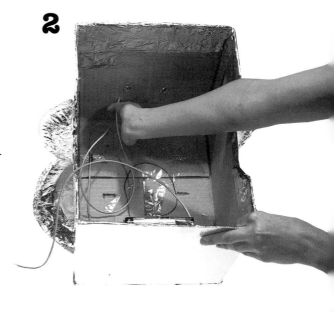

3 Push wire C through the other hole to the front of the box. Wire B will be used later to make the switch.

4 Make a small hole at the top of each eye tube. Insert the bulbs so that the bulb top is above the eye and the glass part is inside. Tape wire A *around* the top of one bulb and wire C *around* the top of the other. Tape wire D *onto* the tops of the bulbs as shown below.

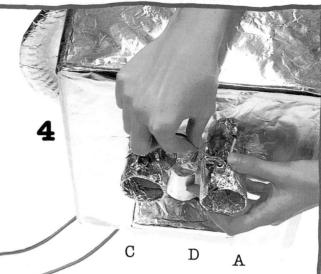

4

B

C   C   D   A

C

5

5 To make the switch, take the ends of wires B and C and attach a paper clip to each. When the paper clips touch, the eyes will light up. If this doesn't happen the first time, make sure that all the connections are secure.

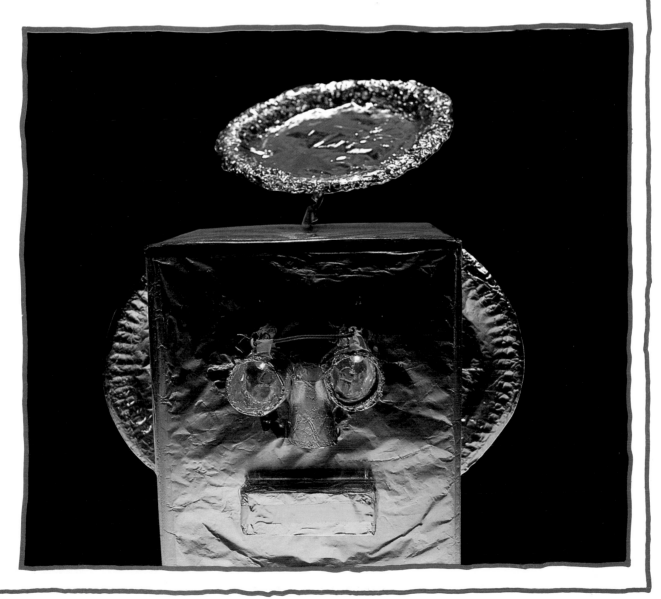

Papier mâché masks

Papier mâché is French for "mashed paper." It is made by soaking paper in paste and then drying it in a particular shape. It's fun to make, but quite messy so be sure to cover your work surface (and your clothes!) before you start. Here we show you how to make a mask shell which can be made into a mouse or an elephant.

What you need
Flour, water, mixing bowl, spoon, strips of newspaper, balloon, and a plastic bowl.

1

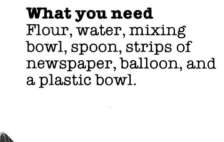

1 Mix enough flour with water to make a thick, creamy paste.

2

2 Stand a large balloon in a plastic bowl to keep it steady. Soak the newspaper strips in paste and cover the balloon with them.

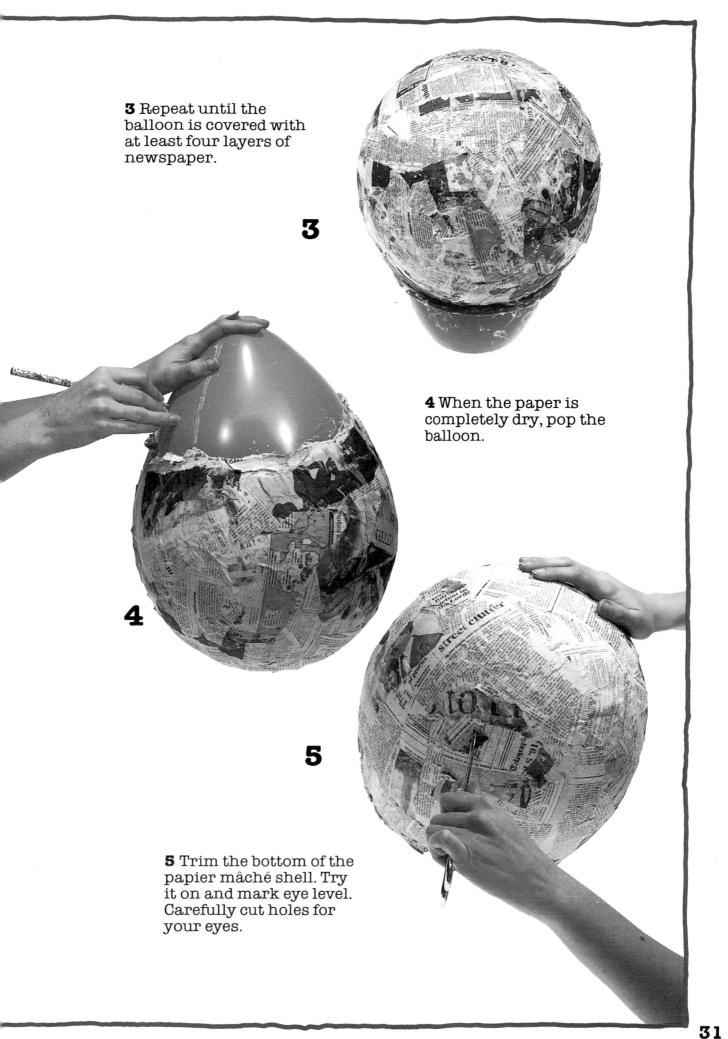

3 Repeat until the balloon is covered with at least four layers of newspaper.

3

4 When the paper is completely dry, pop the balloon.

4

5

5 Trim the bottom of the papier mâché shell. Try it on and mark eye level. Carefully cut holes for your eyes.

Papier mâché

What you need
Brown cardboard, pink paper, 2 strips of cardboard, white paper, egg carton, scissors, glue, paints, and a paintbrush.

The mouse
Paint the papier mâché shell, as shown. Stick on squares of white paper for the teeth. The nose is a section cut from an egg carton.

Make the whiskers by twisting rolls of white paper.

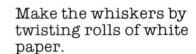

To make the ears curved, make a small cut at the base of each ear. Overlap and glue. Cover each ear with the pink paper shapes. Glue the features to the mouse.

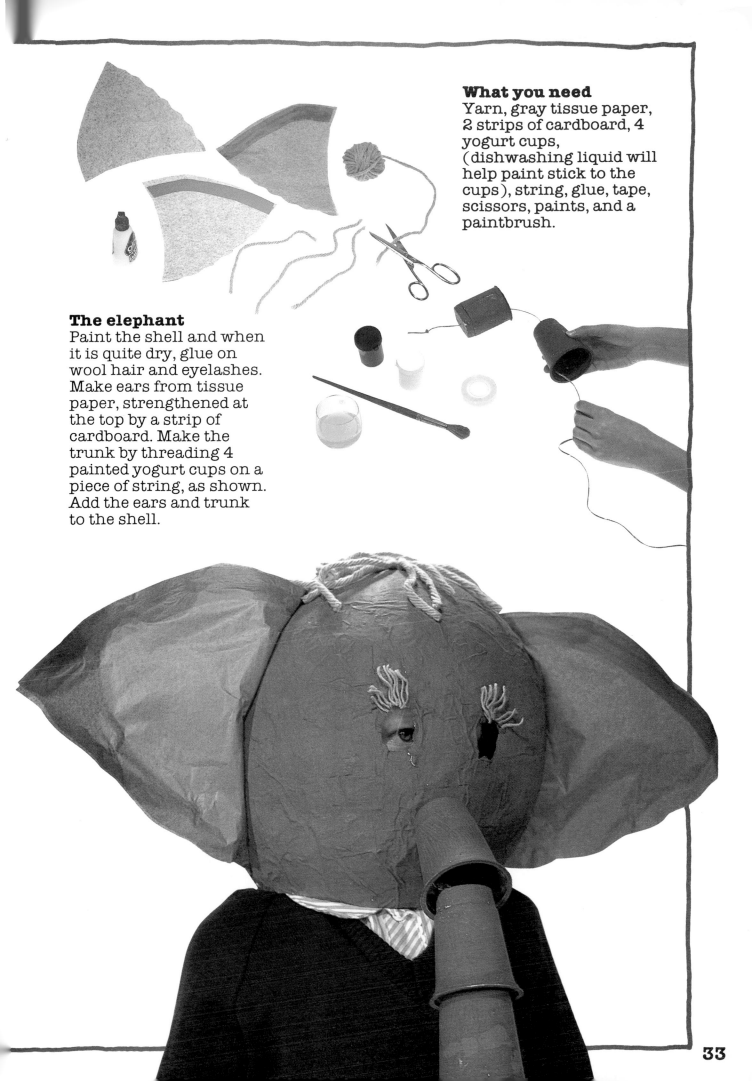

What you need
Yarn, gray tissue paper,
2 strips of cardboard, 4
yogurt cups,
(dishwashing liquid will
help paint stick to the
cups), string, glue, tape,
scissors, paints, and a
paintbrush.

The elephant
Paint the shell and when
it is quite dry, glue on
wool hair and eyelashes.
Make ears from tissue
paper, strengthened at
the top by a strip of
cardboard. Make the
trunk by threading 4
painted yogurt cups on a
piece of string, as shown.
Add the ears and trunk
to the shell.

Bits and pieces

You don't have to wear a complete mask to change your identity. It can be fun just to make various "props" for your face. You could mix them up to create weird and wonderful disguises. The bits and pieces on this page are all worn attached to a circle of cardboard that fits around your head.

For each "prop" you will need a cardboard head-band. Cut a piece of string the size of your head. Make the circle of cardboard using this as a measure.

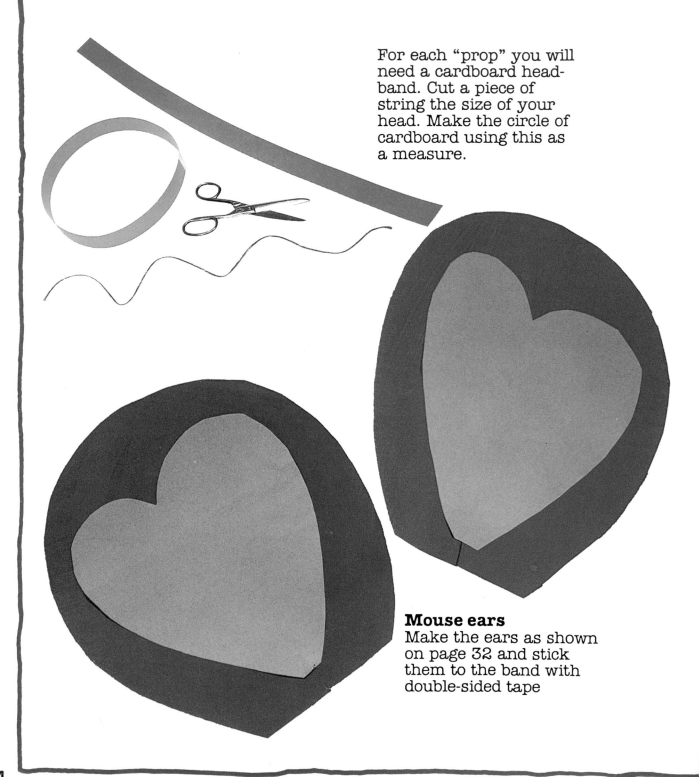

Mouse ears
Make the ears as shown on page 32 and stick them to the band with double-sided tape

King Tut
King Tut is made from just one piece of cardboard and then cleverly painted. Don't forget holes for the eyes.

Clown
The clown's hat and glasses are attached to two separate headbands.

Pirate
This pirate hat and eye patch make a quick and easy fancy dress costume.

Salad faces

More funny faces – this time for eating! Salads make perfect lunches in summer, but prepare them with a bit of imagination and they can look tempting even at partytime. Vary the ingredients each time you make them. Celery, apple, raisins and white cabbage make a change from lettuce and tomato. Experiment with dips to go with the salads – use yogurt or mayonnaise mixed with other ingredients. See the following pages for more fun food ideas.

WHAT YOU NEED
Really fresh vegetables and fruits, such as plums, apples, oranges or bananas (try also mango, kiwi and star fruit), lettuce (there are lots of different kinds to choose from), tomatoes, peppers or scallions, chopping board, sharp knife, two plates.

1

1 Wash and dry the fruits and vegetables. To wash lettuce, first discard the coarse outer leaves, separate the others, wash in cold water and shake dry in a dish towel.

2 Cut up fruit to make the fruity face. Put a damp dish towel under the chopping board to make sure it doesn't slip and use a small sharp knife.

2

FRUITY FACE

3 We have used cheese and a radish for the green man's nose, slices of hard-boiled egg and olives for his eyes, and cheese for hair. You could also roll up ham "curls" for hair.

3

GREEN MAN

1 Sift the flour into a mixing bowl. Add the baking powder, ground ginger and baking soda.

2 Melt the butter, sugar and molasses in a saucepan over a low heat and pour into the flour mixture.

WHAT YOU NEED
1 cup (8 oz) plain flour
1 tsp baking powder
2 tsp ground ginger
½ tsp baking soda
3 oz butter
3 oz brown sugar
2 tbsp molasses
mixing bowl
saucepan
wooden spoon
rolling pin
cutters or sharp knife
spatula
cookie sheet

Ginger cookies

Gingerbread men have been popular cookies for hundreds of years. Stories have even been written about them. You may know the old tale in which the gingerbread man escapes from the oven, shouting:

Run, run as fast as you can,
You can't catch me I'm the gingerbread man!
This recipe shows you how to make about 20 gingerbread characters.

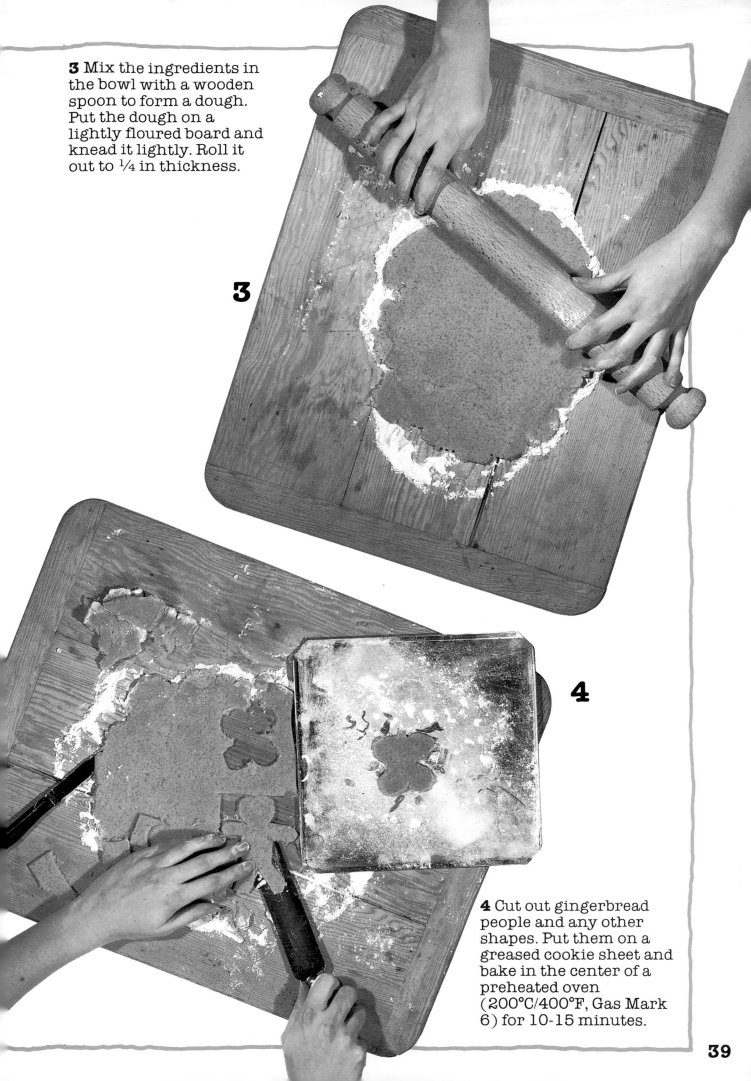

3 Mix the ingredients in the bowl with a wooden spoon to form a dough. Put the dough on a lightly floured board and knead it lightly. Roll it out to ¼ in thickness.

3

4

4 Cut out gingerbread people and any other shapes. Put them on a greased cookie sheet and bake in the center of a preheated oven (200°C/400°F, Gas Mark 6) for 10-15 minutes.

Icing cookies

Traditional gingerbread men have currant eyes and buttons which you add before baking, but it can be fun to decorate your gingerbread shapes with icing. After baking, wait until the cookies are cool and firm and then transfer to a cooling tray where they can become cold and crisp. They are now ready for decorating.

WHAT YOU NEED
powdered sugar
hot water
food coloring
decorations such as:
candied cherries, sprinkles, raisins, chocolate chips, and candy-coated chocolate pieces
a sieve
mixing bowl
spoon and knife

MAKING GLACÉ ICING

1 For each color of icing, sift ¼ cup (2 oz) of powdered sugar into a bowl and add 2 teaspoons of water (or fruit juice). Mix well and add more liquid or powdered sugar, depending on the consistency you want.

2 Add one or two drops of food coloring and mix in well. Use a knife to decorate your shapes. (Keep dipping it in a glass of hot water to make the icing spread smoothly.) Add the other decorations while the icing is still wet so that they stick.

1

2

BUTTERFLY

FISH

CAR

LADYBUG

DOG

RABBIT

GINGERBREAD MAN

41

2

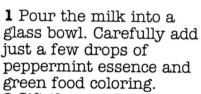

3

4

1 Pour the milk into a glass bowl. Carefully add just a few drops of peppermint essence and green food coloring.
2 Sift the powdered sugar into the bowl and stir until the mixture is quite stiff.
3 Sprinkle some cornflour onto a board. This will stop the mixture from sticking. Put the mixture on the board and knead it until it is smooth.
4 Roll out the mixture to $^1/_4$ in thick sheet.
5 Cut out rounds that are about $^3/_4$ in across.
6 Dip them in melted chocolate, and when the candies are dry wrap them in silver foil.

1

5

PEPPERMINT CREAMS
2 fl oz sweetened condensed milk
peppermint essence
green food coloring
7 oz powdered sugar
cornflour

Peppermint creams **6**

Making candy is one of the nicest aspects of cooking. It's fun, easy and the results are usually delicious. Candies also make perfect presents to give at Christmastime or for birthdays. If you want to give them as gifts, decorate a suitable box, line it with doilies and place wax paper between the layers of candy. This recipe is for peppermint creams, but you could also use it to make lemon creams by substituting lemon flavoring and coloring.

1 Divide the marzipan into 12 pieces. Roll and shape the pieces so that they look like miniature oranges, apples, lemons (pinch the ends to make the lemon shape), pears and bananas.

2 Gently rub the "oranges" and "lemons" on the side of a fine grater to give the markings of lemon and orange peel. Make a dent and put a raisin or clove on each fruit to look like a stalk.

3 Use food dyes to color the fruits.

MARZIPAN FRUITS
¼ cup (2 oz) marzipan
food colorings
raisins or cloves

Marzipan treats

Here we show you how to make marzipan fruits. You could also try marzipan whirls. First divide the marzipan into three. Work different food colorings into two of the parts, a drop at a time. Roll each piece out flat and then sandwich the three parts together. Roll up the "sandwich" into a sausage shape and cut off slices to make the individual candies.

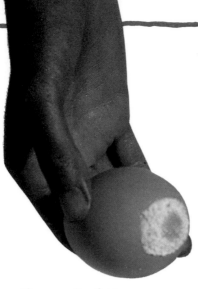

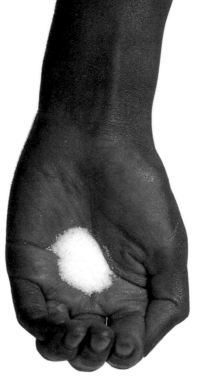

1 Moisten the end of the egg. As you joke with your audience, gently turn the egg in the salt you have hidden in your hand.

The educated egg

The educated egg is not for eating, it's for entertaining your friends. This is a very simple but effective piece of magic. Ask your audience to try to balance an egg on one end. After watching them all fail, you say your magic words and the egg balances perfectly!

The secret of the trick

The trick is to secretly cover the base of the egg in some salt. Instead of rolling over, as it did for the audience, its salted base will make the egg stay upright.

2 Say your magic words and slowly set the egg upright on the table. Brush your hands together (to get rid of the secret salt) and say "Presto!"

2

BEFORE YOU START
Dissolve some sea salt in a glass of warm water. Place it next to a glass containing ordinary water. Take care to remember which is which.

Eggs-periment!

In this trick you make two identical eggs behave in completely different ways. One egg will sink in a glass of water, while an identical egg will stay afloat!

The secret of the trick
Although they look the same, one of the tumblers of water actually contains a solution of sea salt which makes the egg float.

1 Ask someone to pick any two eggs from a bowl. Say which will sink and which will float.

2 Carefully put the eggs into the correct glasses and take your applause!

1   **2**

Handy magic

In this trick, you appear to perform the extraordinary feat of pushing a coin right through your hand!

The secret of the trick

This piece of magic depends on "sleight-of-hand." Sleights are secret movements of your hands that are not seen by the audience. Consequently your audience thinks you are doing one thing, when you are really doing another. Sleights are very useful for making tricks work, but to be successful the movements must be smooth and natural.

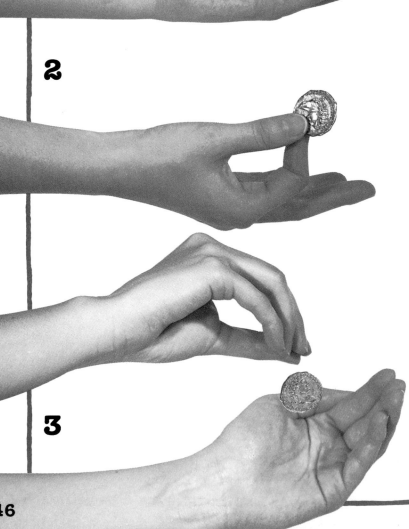

1

1 After showing your audience that your left hand is empty, attempt to "push" the coin through the back of your hand.

2

2 With a puzzled frown, open your hands and admit to the audience that it isn't working and that you will try harder.

3

3 This is where the sleight-of-hand comes in. Before you close your left hand to try again, secretly drop the coin from your right hand into your left.

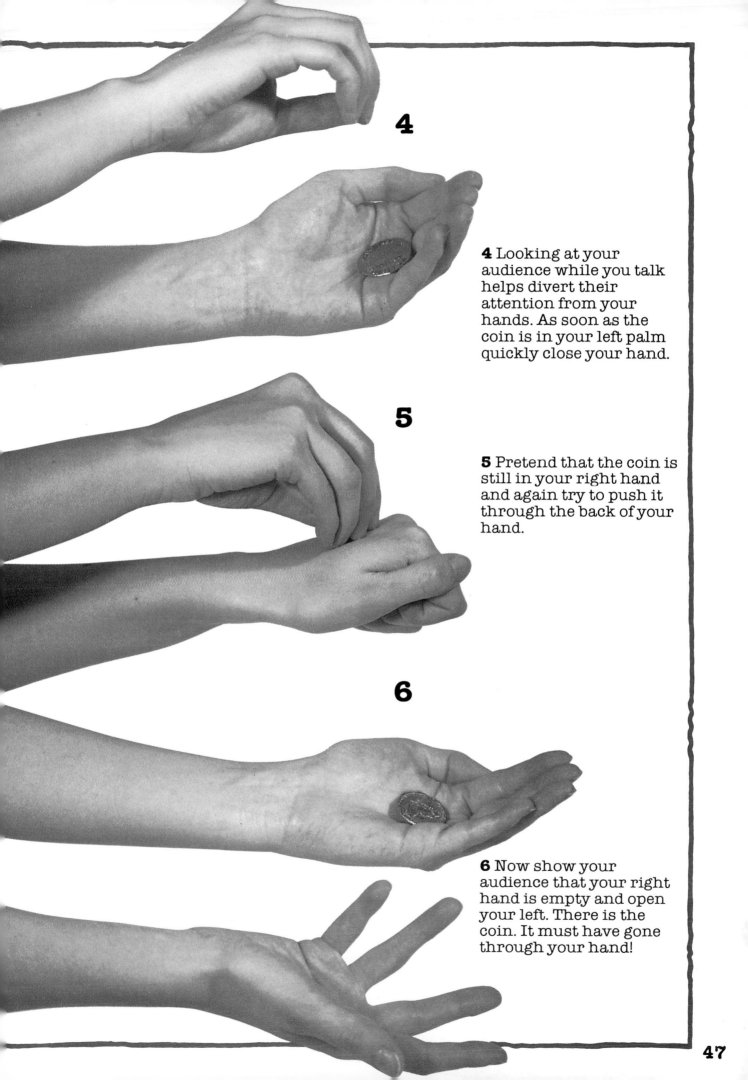

4 Looking at your audience while you talk helps divert their attention from your hands. As soon as the coin is in your left palm quickly close your hand.

5 Pretend that the coin is still in your right hand and again try to push it through the back of your hand.

6 Now show your audience that your right hand is empty and open your left. There is the coin. It must have gone through your hand!

BEFORE YOU START
Line a cardboard box with soft materials that will cushion the sound of the glass falling. Place the box behind the magician's table.

1

1 Tell your audience you will make a coin disappear with the aid of a tumbler, but as it has to be secret, you must cover the tumbler with paper.

The vanishing glass

In this trick, you announce to the audience that you are going to make a coin disappear with the aid of a glass tumbler. Mysteriously the coin remains, but the glass tumbler disappears in front of their very eyes!

The secret of the trick
This trick depends on your convincing the audience that the glass is still in a piece of paper, when in fact you have secretly dropped it into a box behind the magician's table. The coin is there to fool the eye, and it will distract the audience's attention away from your secret moves. This is called "misdirection."

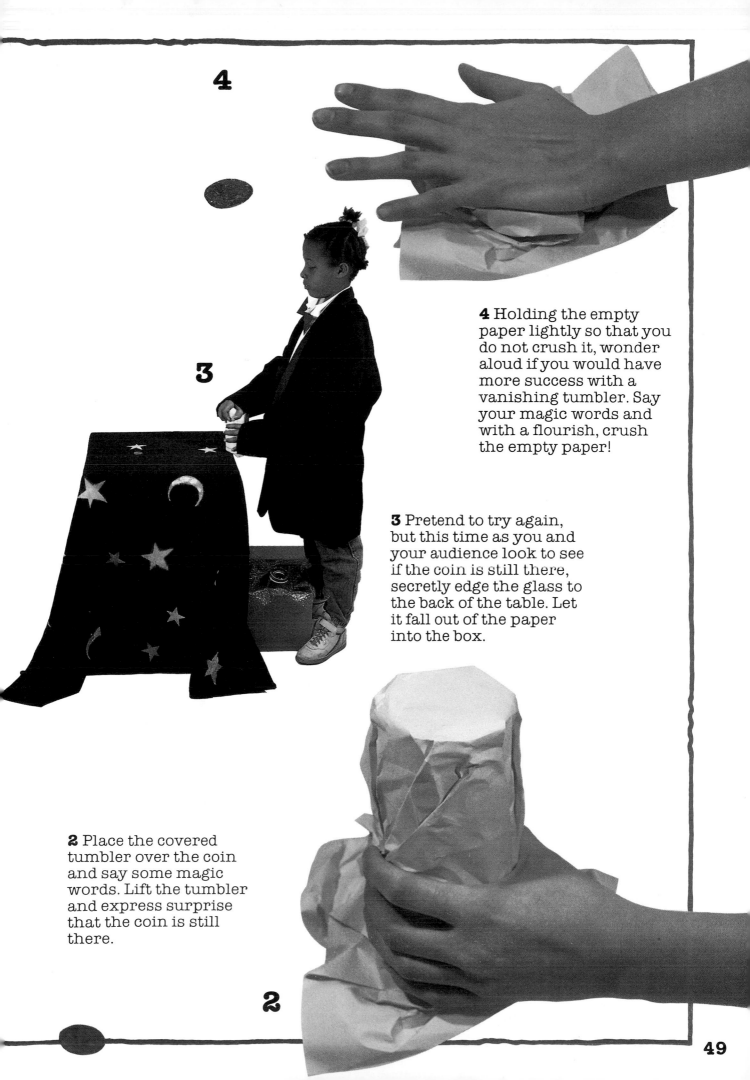

4

4 Holding the empty paper lightly so that you do not crush it, wonder aloud if you would have more success with a vanishing tumbler. Say your magic words and with a flourish, crush the empty paper!

3

3 Pretend to try again, but this time as you and your audience look to see if the coin is still there, secretly edge the glass to the back of the table. Let it fall out of the paper into the box.

2 Place the covered tumbler over the coin and say some magic words. Lift the tumbler and express surprise that the coin is still there.

2

Magic cord

This trick is a little more complicated, but it is worth the effort just to see your spectators' astonished faces. With the aid of some magic words, you make a scarf and rings fly through a length of cord.

The secret of the trick

Unknown to your audience, you arrange the cords in such a way that they are not what they seem.

BEFORE YOU START
Tie two cords at the center with a piece of thread.

1

1 Ask two volunteers to pull on the cords while you hide the secret thread.

2

2 Ask them to examine the rings and scarf as you secretly arrange the cords as shown.

3

4 Unknown to them, each volunteer is now holding *both* ends of one cord. Tie two of the ends together.

4

3 Tie the scarf at the center to hide the thread. Ask the volunteers to thread the rings onto their ends of the cords.

5 Now ask the volunteers to pull hard. The secret thread will break and the rings and scarf will fly off as if by magic!

Famous people

The magic here is all about mind reading. You amaze your audience by correctly predicting the name of a famous personality they have chosen.

The secret of the trick

This clever trick depends on your convincing the audience that you have done one thing, when you have really done another. You will need to use good misdirection to prevent them from suspecting the trick.

1 Ask your audience to call out names of famous people. Pretend to write each name on a piece of paper, but really just continue to write the first name given. Ask how to spell the names to keep the audience from suspecting.

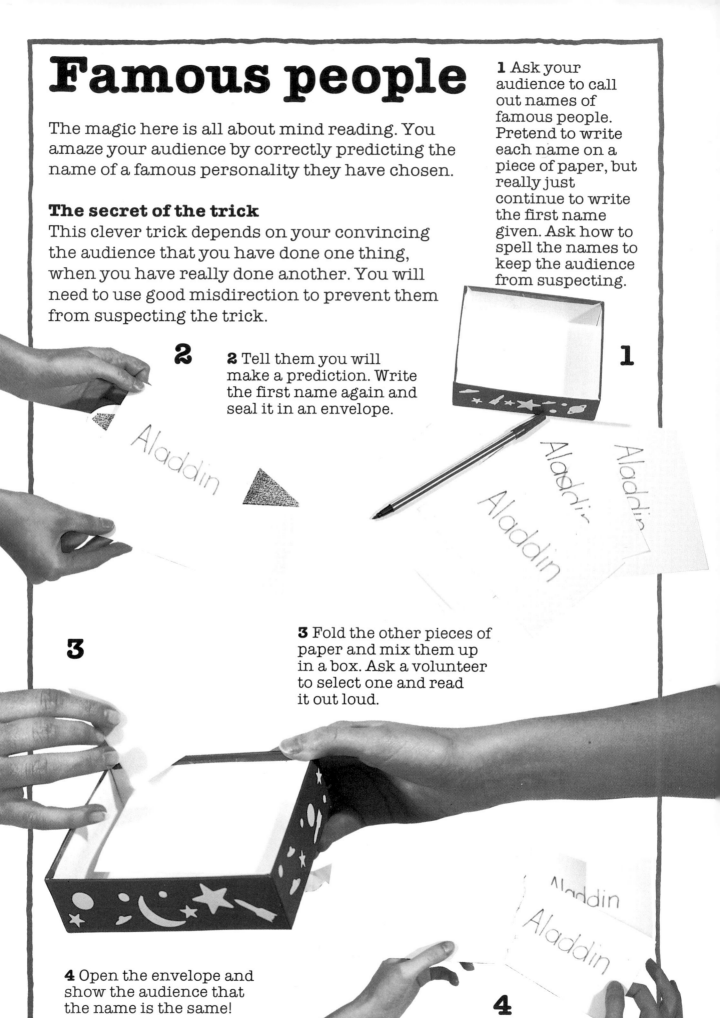

2 Tell them you will make a prediction. Write the first name again and seal it in an envelope.

3 Fold the other pieces of paper and mix them up in a box. Ask a volunteer to select one and read it out loud.

4 Open the envelope and show the audience that the name is the same!

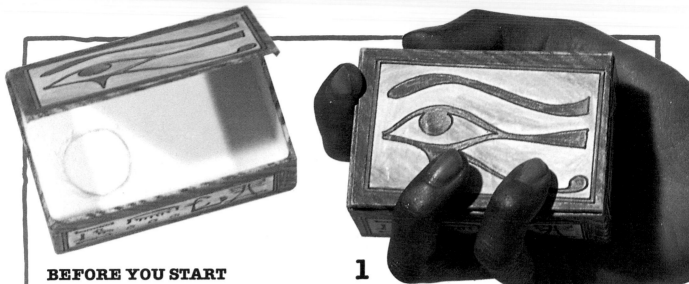

BEFORE YOU START
First take a box with a lid and decorate it to suit your story. Line it with cotton balls. Spot it with red paint if your story involves a recently severed finger!

1

1 Holding the box in your hand and with your finger through the hole, tell your audience your gory tale.

2

Pharaoh's finger

In this wonderfully gruesome piece of magic, you show your audience an ancient box containing a mummified human finger.

The secret of the trick
The trick is simple — there is a hole in the bottom of the box and the finger is your own. But with a good presentation and a lot of acting you can completely convince your audience. Rehearse an elaborate story of how you acquired the box, perhaps from your great uncle who was an archaeologist in Egypt. Dusting your finger with talcum powder will produce a macabre effect!

2 Extend your arm and slowly lift the lid to reveal the finger. You can even invite members of the audience to touch it, after suggesting how clammy and ancient it feels! Return the box to a safe place while the audience is still very interested.

Levitation

In this spectacular feat of magic, you perform the impossible. Using a few carefully chosen magic words and a magic wand, you make your assistant rise completely off the ground!

The secret of the trick
Of course your assistant doesn't really leave the ground completely. Unseen by the audience he changes position and so is able to raise himself, creating the illusion of levitation. Like many simple tricks, you need a good, confident performance to convince the audience. Practice with your assistant until the movements are smooth and natural.

2 Put the cloth in front of your assistant and slowly cover him with it. As this is happening, the assistant quickly and smoothly moves from his back to his front, unseen by the audience.

1 Introduce yourself as a master of levitation and show the audience that your magic cloth conceals no hidden devices. Ask your assistant to lie on his back on the floor.

3 Create an atmosphere by asking for silence as the next stage demands intense concentration. Chant your magic words and raise your hands above your assistant's body.

3

5

4 At a prearranged cue, your assistant slowly and steadily raises his body as shown.

4

5 For maximum effect, he should try to make a straight line with his body. As the spectators think he is on his back, they will be stunned by what they see!

Swordbox

In this ever popular piece of magic you place your assistant in a box into which you then thrust several swords. Despite moans and groans, your assistant finally emerges miraculously unscathed!

The secret of the trick

This trick depends on two facts which are not known to the audience. The first is that the assistant doesn't sit in the position they think she is in and the second is that the sword holes have already been carefully arranged in advance. It involves quite a lot of preparation, but the more trouble you take, the more impressive it will be.

BEFORE YOU START
Decorate a box big enough for your assistant to sit in. While she is facing outward, carefully make holes so that the cardboard swords fit around her.

1 After showing the audience the inside of the box, your assistant gets in and sits facing the back of the box. Turn the box around and at the same time the assistant moves to the pre-arranged position. Begin to thrust the swords through the prepared holes.

2 If your assistant was facing the audience, as the spectators believe, the swords would be going right through her. Instead she is helping to guide the swords through the correct holes.

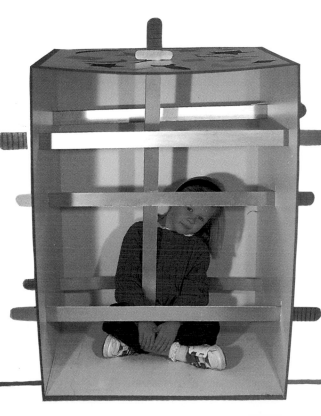

FINALE
After your assistant's moans have died down, remove the swords one by one. Your assistant can then leap from the box unharmed to the applause of the audience!

57

Ribbon magic

This trick will mystify your audience. You cut a ribbon in half and then, with the aid of your magic wand, you transform the two pieces back into a whole piece again.

The secret of the trick

The secret here is that you have something up your sleeve! Unknown to your audience, you actually have two pieces of ribbon. The piece which is cut conveniently disappears up your sleeve, leaving the whole piece of ribbon in front of your audience's astonished faces.

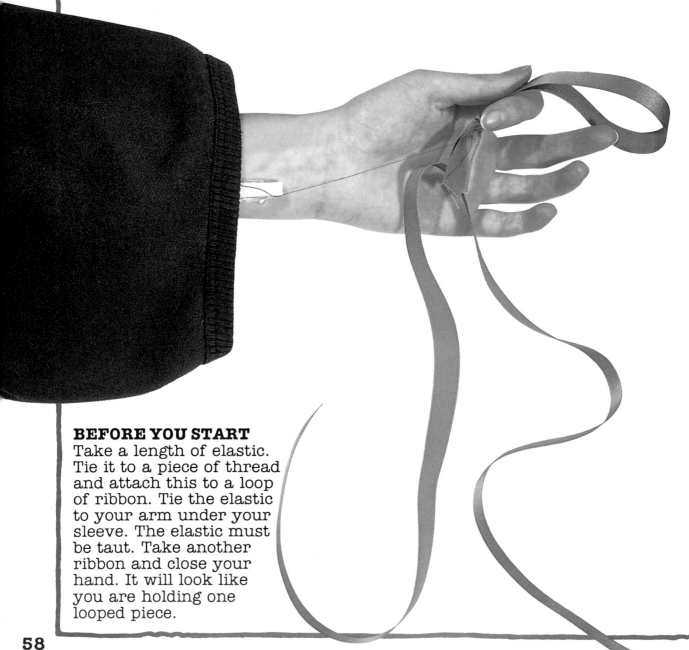

BEFORE YOU START
Take a length of elastic. Tie it to a piece of thread and attach this to a loop of ribbon. Tie the elastic to your arm under your sleeve. The elastic must be taut. Take another ribbon and close your hand. It will look like you are holding one looped piece.

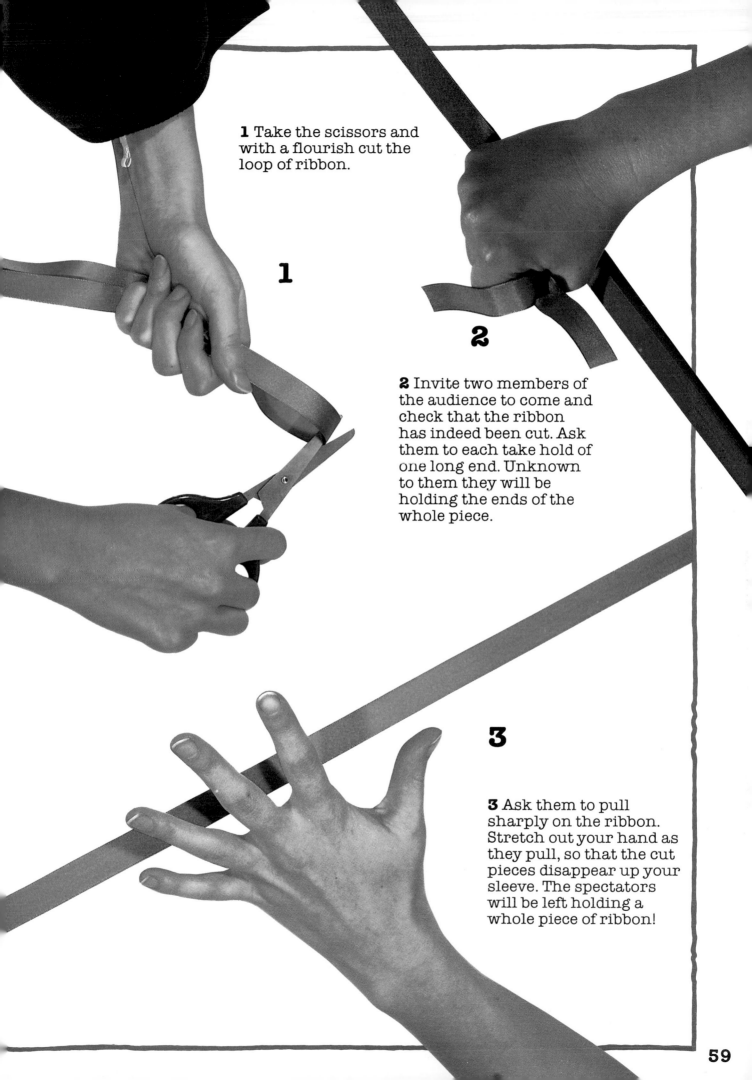

1 Take the scissors and with a flourish cut the loop of ribbon.

1

2

2 Invite two members of the audience to come and check that the ribbon has indeed been cut. Ask them to each take hold of one long end. Unknown to them they will be holding the ends of the whole piece.

3

3 Ask them to pull sharply on the ribbon. Stretch out your hand as they pull, so that the cut pieces disappear up your sleeve. The spectators will be left holding a whole piece of ribbon!

Spot the dot

Many of these card tricks involve the card magician in mysteriously identifying a card chosen by a member of the audience. In each case the presentation and method are different, so that what the audience actually sees is a wide variety of exciting tricks. This is one of the more simple examples.

The secret of the trick

The secret here is that there is a pencil line along the side of the deck of cards. It will not be noticed by the audience, but it allows you to identify the chosen card.

BEFORE YOU START

Draw a line across the side of the deck of cards as shown. Use a soft pencil as this will make a wide mark and it will be easily erased.

1 Ask a spectator to pick a card. You must not be able to see the card.

1

2 Tell the spectator to memorize the card and replace it anywhere in the deck.

2

3 While you talk to the audience, glance at the cards. The chosen card will show up as a small pencil dot in the side of the deck.

3

4 Pick out the chosen card and, with a flourish, present it to the audience.

4

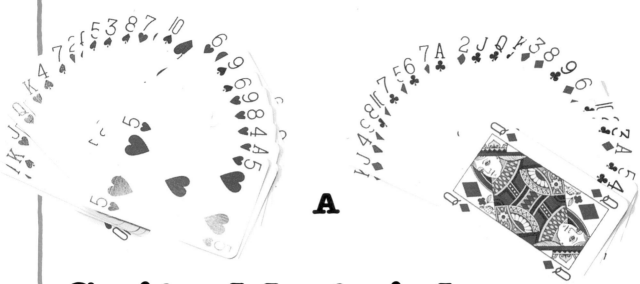

A

Suit-able trickery

In this trick you astonish your audience once more by finding a card that was chosen and then replaced at random in the pack.

The secret of the trick
What the spectators don't realize is that you have carefully prepared the pack in advance so that the replacement of the chosen card is not as random as it seems.

BEFORE YOU START (A)
Sort the pack into two halves, one containing spades and hearts, the other with diamonds and clubs. The audience will not notice this arrangement because the cards will still be a mixture of blacks and reds.

B

1

BEFORE YOU START (B)
Now put the two halves together so that the top card of the bottom half sticks out slightly. This will be a marker between the top and bottom halves.

1 Divide the cards into two halves, using the marker card as a guide. Show the audience the cards. The division will look random, but you will have your two carefully arranged halves.

2

2 Ask someone to "pick a card, any card" from one half of the pack. In our photograph the cards are visible, but of course the card magician must not see which card has been chosen.

3

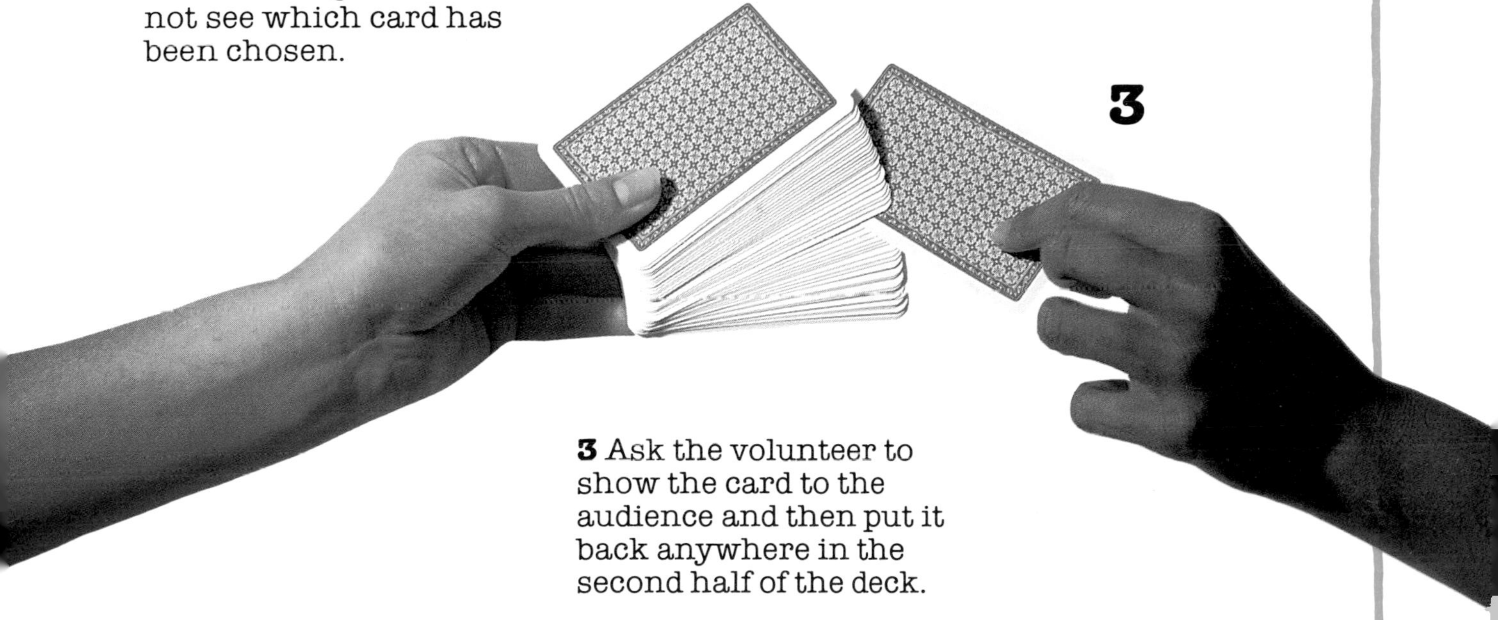

3 Ask the volunteer to show the card to the audience and then put it back anywhere in the second half of the deck.

4

4 Sort through the cards. The chosen card will be immediately obvious because it will be the only one of that suit. Show your audience the card and take your applause!

Crafty glimpse

This trick shows another way of identifying a card chosen and replaced by your audience. Once you have perfected this simple method, you can use it to make up your own card tricks.

The secret of the trick

The secret of this trick is that you have taken a crafty glimpse at the bottom card while your audience's attention was elsewhere. By arranging the cards in a particular way, this glimpse enables you to identify the chosen card.

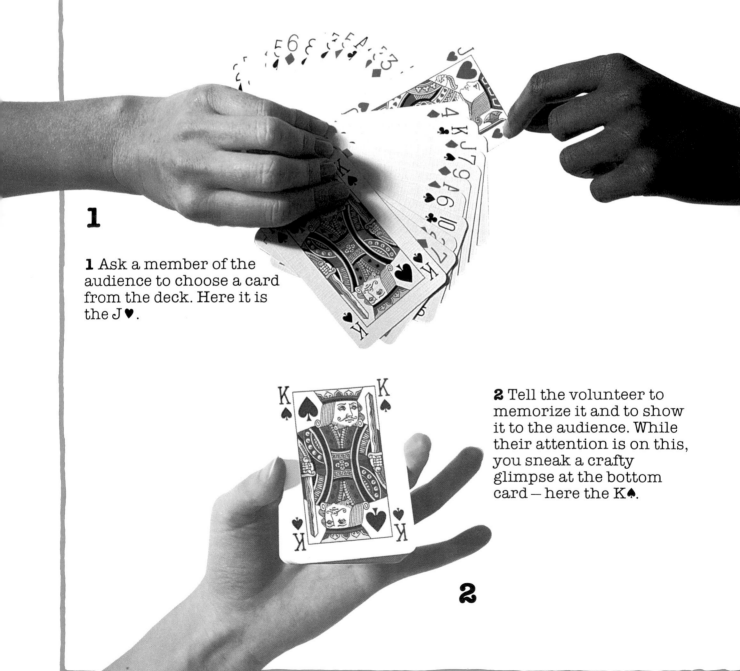

1

1 Ask a member of the audience to choose a card from the deck. Here it is the J ♥.

2 Tell the volunteer to memorize it and to show it to the audience. While their attention is on this, you sneak a crafty glimpse at the bottom card — here the K ♠.

2

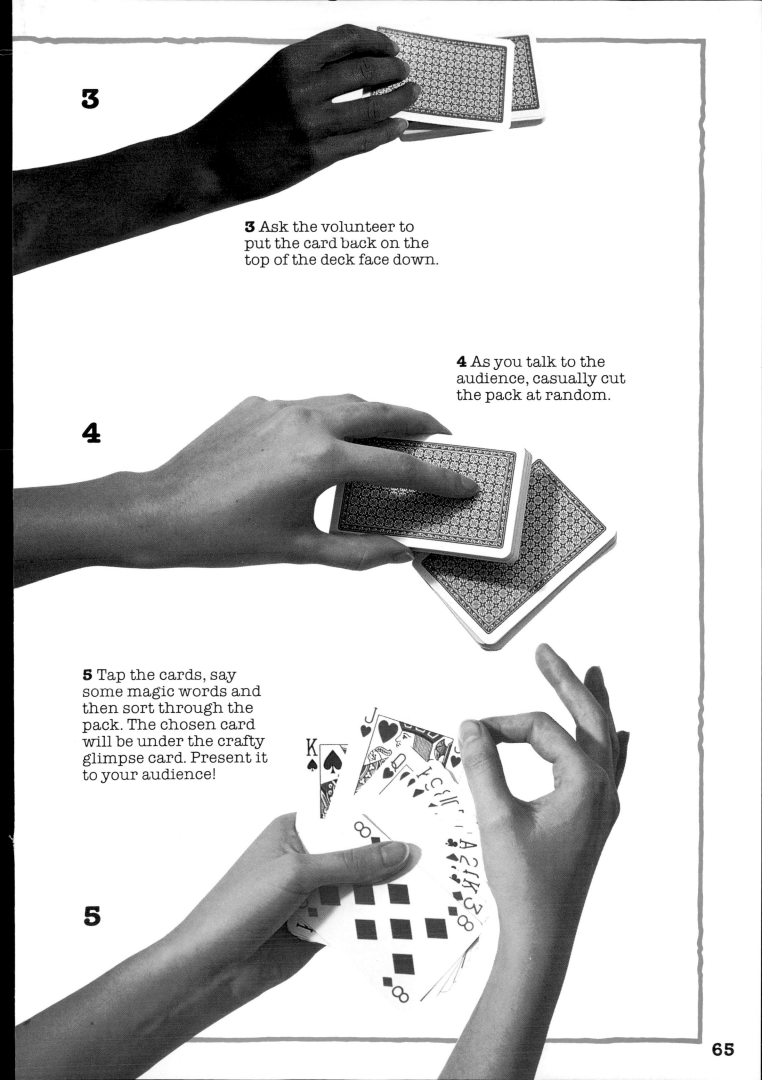

3 Ask the volunteer to put the card back on the top of the deck face down.

4 As you talk to the audience, casually cut the pack at random.

5 Tap the cards, say some magic words and then sort through the pack. The chosen card will be under the crafty glimpse card. Present it to your audience!

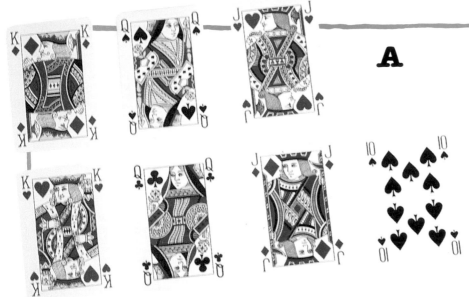

A

BEFORE YOU START (A)

Rehearse your story so that you can give a confident presentation. Pick out the two red Kings, black Queens, red Jacks and one ten.

Burning building

This trick is great fun to do. It involves a story that you act out with the cards. Members of a royal family escape from a burning building and miraculously they move from the middle to the bottom of the pack.

The secret of the trick

This crafty trick relies on a little preparation of the deck before your audience arrives.

B

1 Explain to your audience that the deck is the royal building. The King lives at the top of the building. Place the K♥ in the deck near the top.

1

BEFORE YOU START (B)

Put the K♦, Q♠ and J♥ at the bottom of the pack in that order. You will use the remaining cards to tell your story.

66

2 The Queen lives on the next floor down. Place the Q♣ halfway down.

3 The Jack lives on the floor below this. Place the J♦ near the bottom.

4 The servant — the 10♠ — lives right at the bottom. Put this card on the bottom of the pack. Tell the audience how a fire breaks out in the building.

5 Luckily there is a fire escape and the family is able to descend to the street. Turn over the royal cards at the bottom of the deck. Your audience will be amazed!

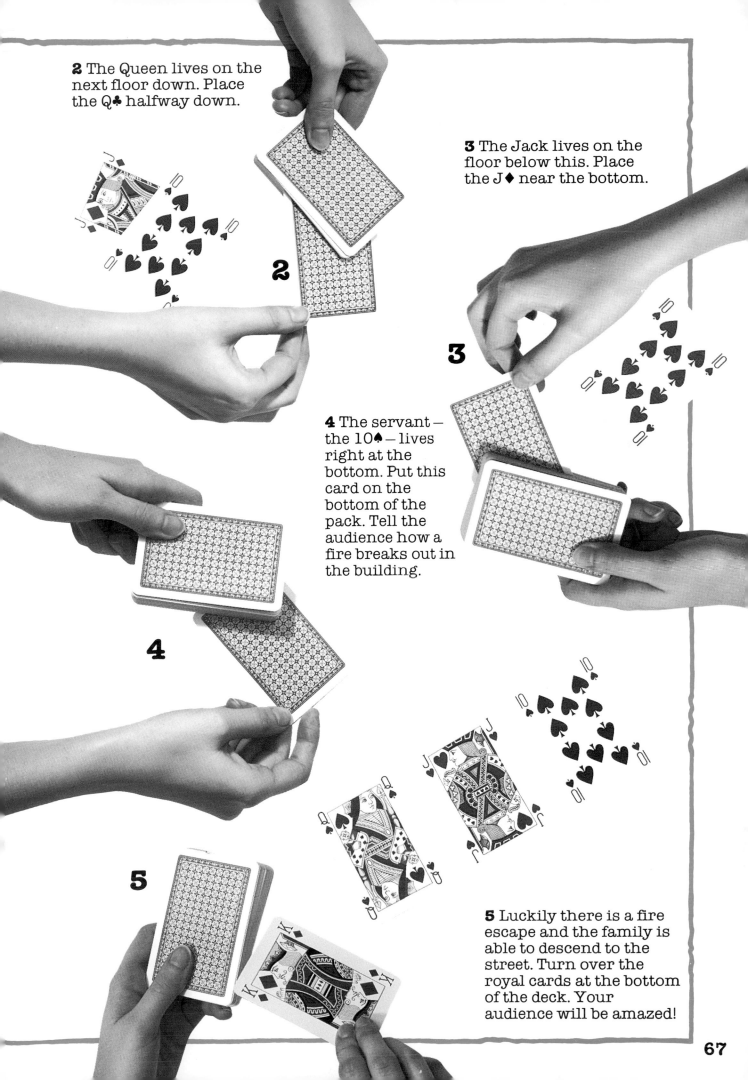

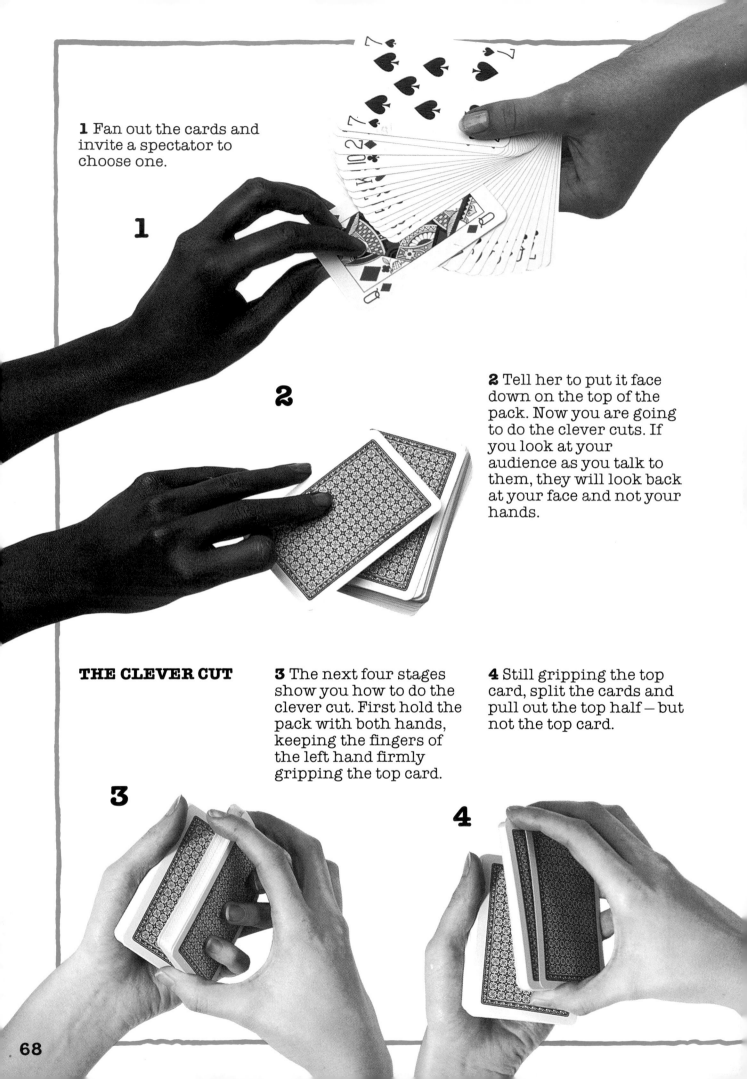

1 Fan out the cards and invite a spectator to choose one.

2 Tell her to put it face down on the top of the pack. Now you are going to do the clever cuts. If you look at your audience as you talk to them, they will look back at your face and not your hands.

THE CLEVER CUT

3 The next four stages show you how to do the clever cut. First hold the pack with both hands, keeping the fingers of the left hand firmly gripping the top card.

4 Still gripping the top card, split the cards and pull out the top half — but not the top card.

Clever cut

In this trick a spectator places her chosen card on the top of the deck and no matter how many times you cut the pack, the card magically remains at the top!

The secret of the trick

The magic here is created by handling the cards in a such way that the cuts appear genuine, but they leave the top card in the same position. You will need to practice this well to be convincing.

8 Turn over the top card. Your audience should be astonished. It is the chosen card.

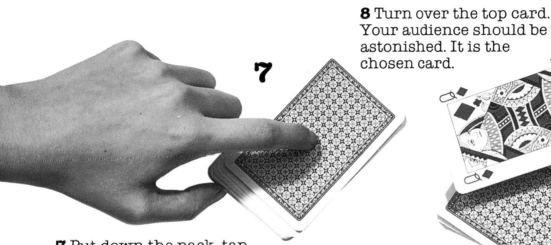

7 Put down the pack, tap it or perhaps say a few magic words.

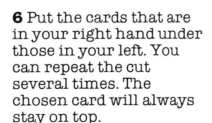

5 The chosen card will still be the top card in your left hand.

6 Put the cards that are in your right hand under those in your left. You can repeat the cut several times. The chosen card will always stay on top.

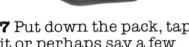
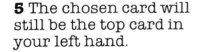

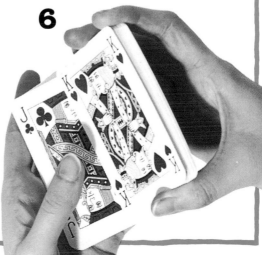

ABRACADABRA

No matter how sharp your spectators are, they will never guess how you identified the chosen card in this clever trick.

The secret of the trick

This trick appears to work all by itself! In fact it relies on a numerical arrangement of the cards, but all the card magician has to remember are the following simple stages.

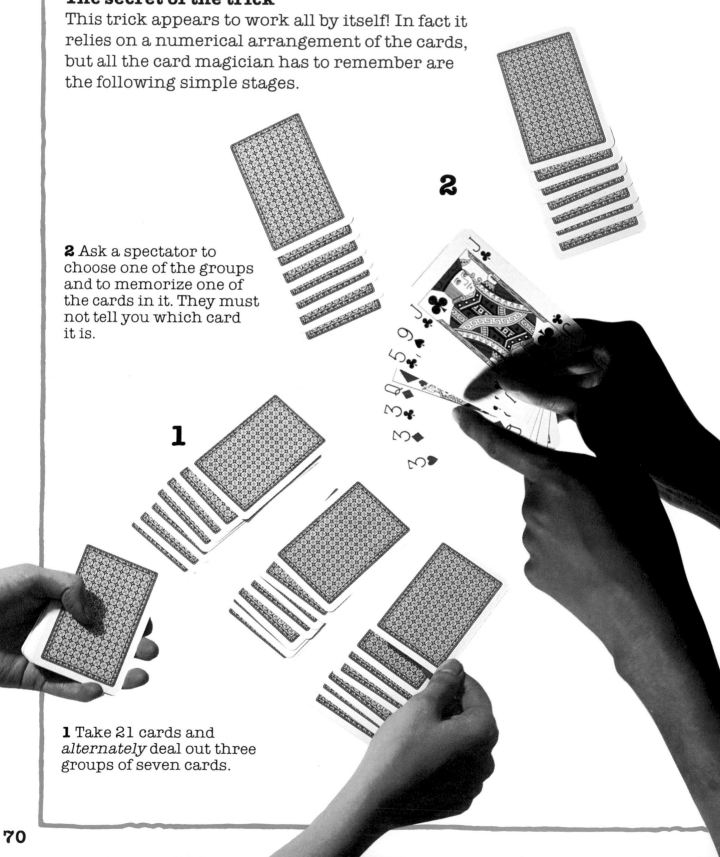

2 Ask a spectator to choose one of the groups and to memorize one of the cards in it. They must not tell you which card it is.

1 Take 21 cards and *alternately* deal out three groups of seven cards.

3 Tell the spectator to replace the group of cards.

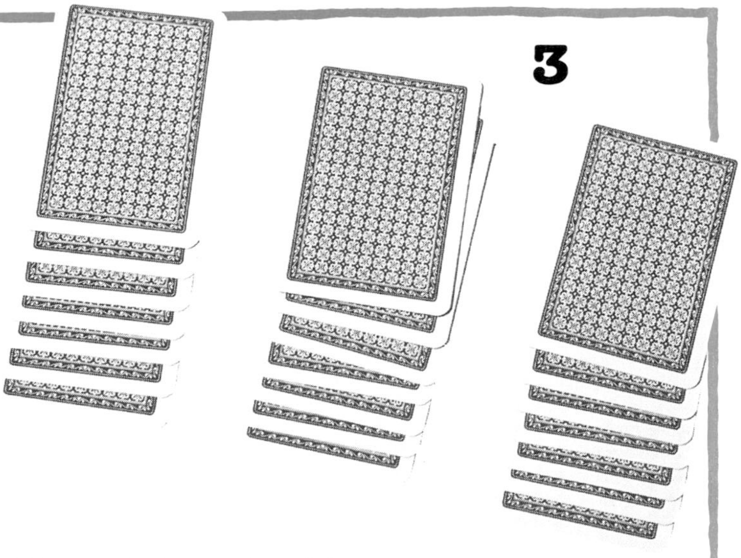

3

4 Gather up the three groups, taking care to put the chosen group in the middle.

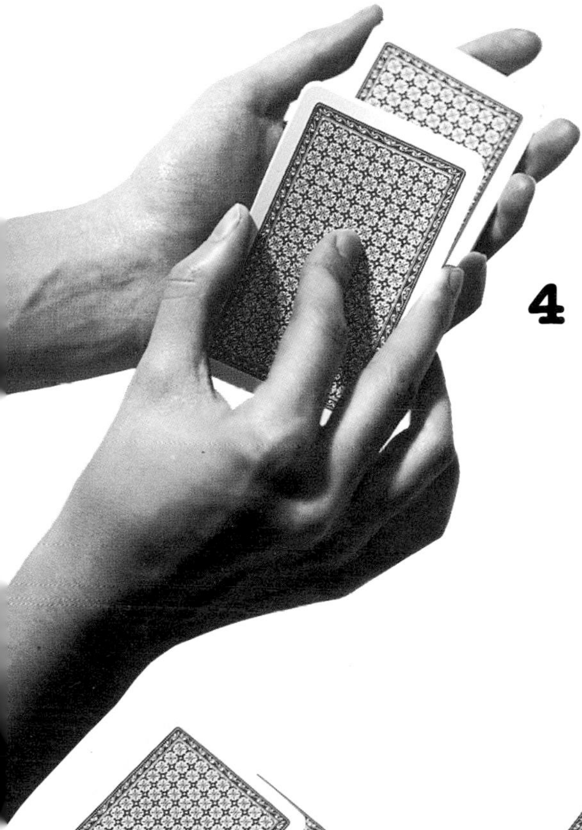

4

5 Repeat stages 1 – 4 two more times, taking care to gather up the cards so that the group containing the chosen card is always in the middle.

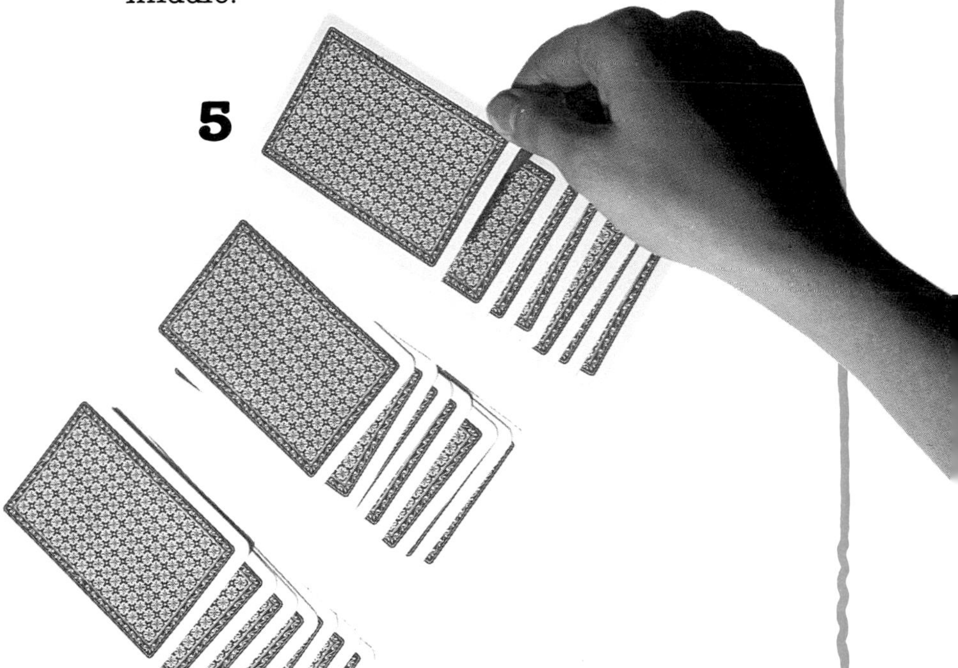

5

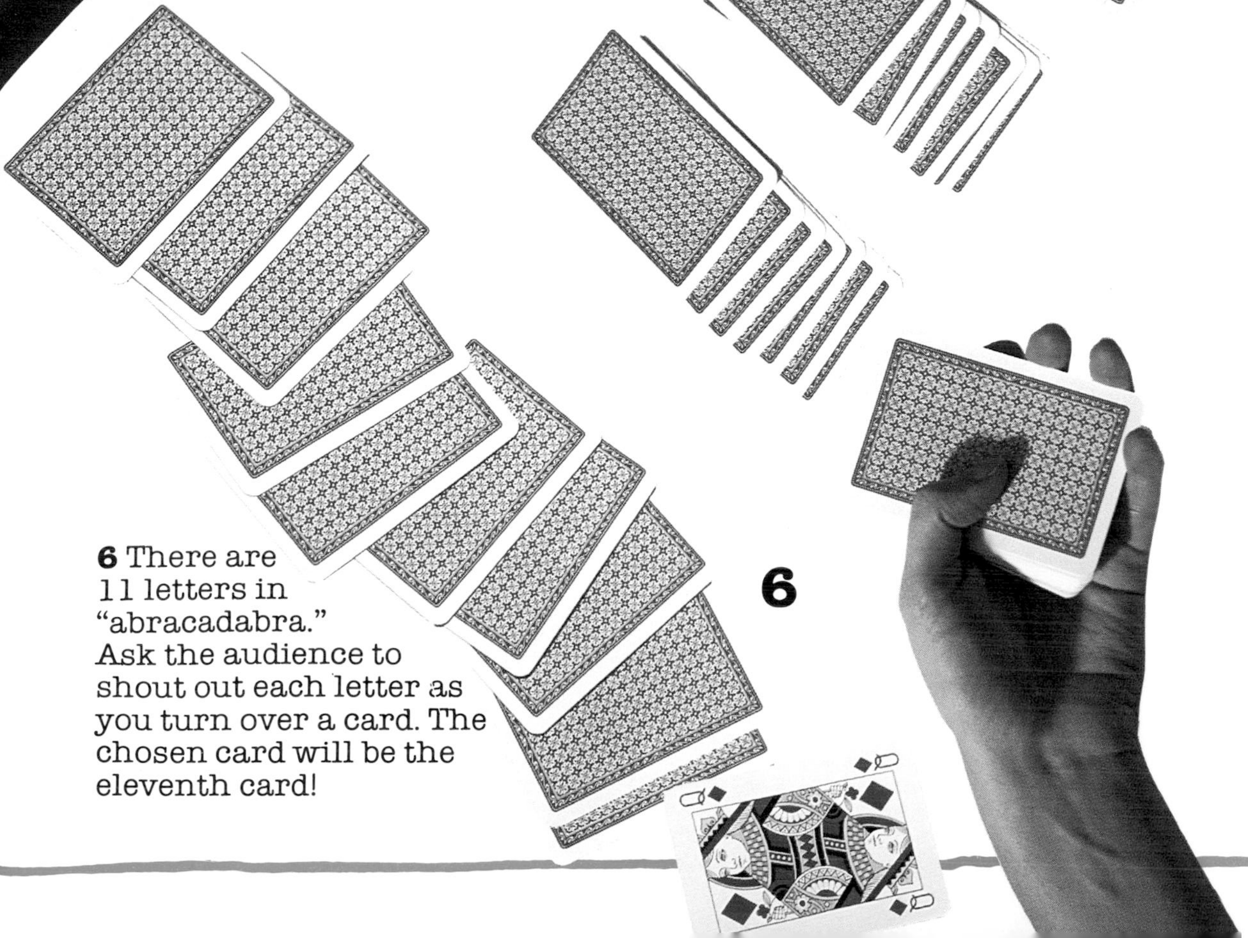

6 There are 11 letters in "abracadabra." Ask the audience to shout out each letter as you turn over a card. The chosen card will be the eleventh card!

6

Dancing Dandy

Dancing Dandy is a puppet toy, rather than a puppet that acts in a puppet theater. You can have fun making him for yourself or you could make him to give as a present. Once you have mastered the Dancing Dandy, you can use the same idea to make other dancing puppet toys, such as a ballerina or a clown. Copy the Dancing Dandy carefully from the pictures shown here or make up your own.

You will need cardboard, string, brass paper fasteners, scotch tape or strong glue, paints or felt-tip pens to decorate.

HOW TO WORK THE DANDY
Hold the string at the top and bottom of the puppet. Gently pull and release the string so that the arms and legs dance in and out.

1 Trace the pattern shapes onto thin cardboard and carefully cut them out. Decorate and make holes for the string and fasteners as shown.

2 Put the Dandy together with paper fasteners, making sure that his arms and legs can move freely.

3 Use fine string to join the arms together and the legs together.

4 Attach a string to the head. With the arms and legs in the outstretched position, tie another piece of string to link the arms and legs.

Swinging monkey

Like the Dancing Dandy, the swinging monkey is a puppet toy. He's quite easy to make, yet his acrobatics are very impressive. If you design your own monkey, make sure his arms are longer than his body.

You will need cardboard, two sticks, string, a paper fastener, glue, two sections cut from a drinking straw, paints or felt-tip pens.

HOW THE MONKEY WORKS
Hold a stick in each hand. Move the tops of the sticks away from each other and the monkey will swing up. As he reaches the top, move the sticks together slightly and he will swing over. Repeat this and the monkey will swing over backward.

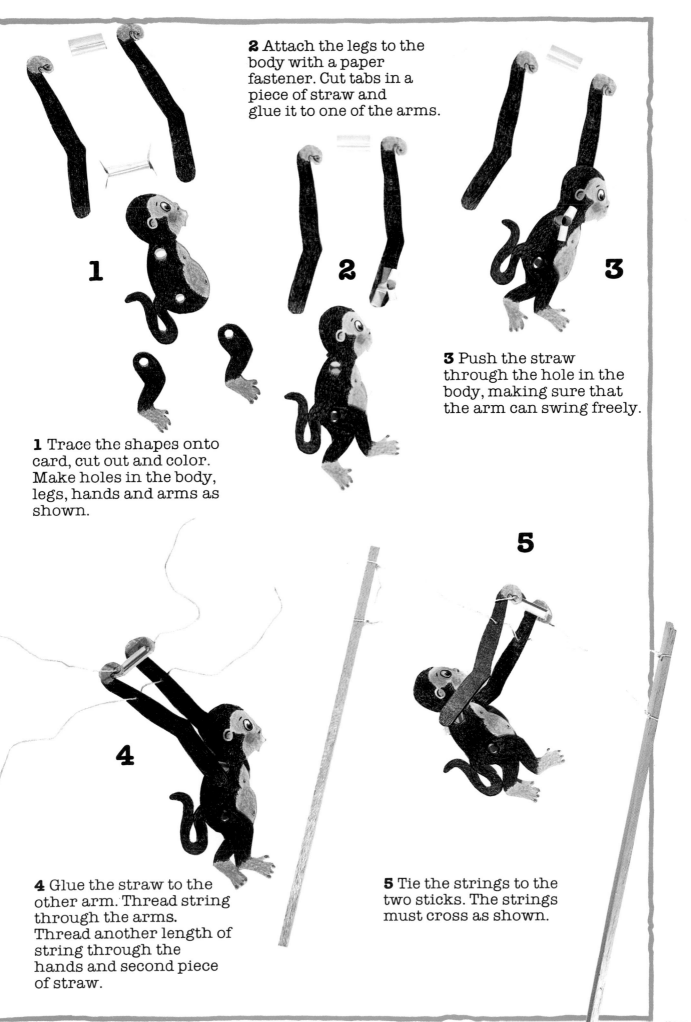

1 Trace the shapes onto card, cut out and color. Make holes in the body, legs, hands and arms as shown.

2 Attach the legs to the body with a paper fastener. Cut tabs in a piece of straw and glue it to one of the arms.

3 Push the straw through the hole in the body, making sure that the arm can swing freely.

4 Glue the straw to the other arm. Thread string through the arms. Thread another length of string through the hands and second piece of straw.

5 Tie the strings to the two sticks. The strings must cross as shown.

Glove puppets

Glove puppets are very easy to make and they are also excellent performers in a puppet show. They can pick up props and suggest a wide range of moods by using their hands and arms. You don't have to cut up your gloves to make these puppets as you use an old sock for the head and body.

You will need gloves, old socks, yarn, cotton balls, colored felt, string, paper, glue, gummed labels and felt-tip pens.

HOW GLOVE PUPPETS WORK
Put your gloved hand in the sock so that your forefinger is in the head and your middle finger and thumb become the arms. The puppet can twist its body, bow, nod its head, clap hands and pick up props.

PATRICIA PANDA

KEVIN THE CLOWN
This jolly circus character is brightly colored, with his blue body, green hair and yellow hat. His big red nose is a cotton ball.

ANGRY ANDY
This fearsome fellow looks mean and moody. His wild black yarn hair is stuck out with hairspray.

FIONA FAIRFLAX
The fair Fiona has been given a startled expression with gummed label eyes and mouth.

77

How to make Fiona Fairflax

You need a pink sock and glove for Fiona's body and arms, yellow yarn for her hair, string, paper, yarn, gummed labels and felt-tip pens.

1

1 Cut several lengths of yarn and tie at one end with string. Cut a hole in the sock. Push the tied end of the yarn into the hole and tie a piece of string around the sock to secure it.

78

2 Scrunch up a ball of paper, leaving a hole in which to put your finger. Put the ball in the sock and tie loosely with yarn.

2

3

3 Make Fiona's face from gummed labels and use black yarn to make her eyelashes.

4 Cut holes in either side of the sock where you think her arms should go. You can cover the holes with strips of felt.

4

5

5 Trim hair to style, put on the glove and Fiona is ready!

Stick puppets

This strange band of musicians with their conductor are all stick puppets. You can make this kind of puppet as complicated or as simple as you like. Our puppets each have two sticks, with one stick operating an arm and one supporting the body. You can make stick puppets with many moving parts – although you may need an assistant or two to help you operate them.

You will need dowels, balsa wood or garden stakes, (long pencils can also be used), colored felt, drawing pins, yarn, cotton balls or ping-pong balls, plasticine, cardboard and pens.

HOW STICK PUPPETS WORK
These puppets are very simple to operate. You hold the stick that supports the body with one hand, while moving the other stick around so that the puppet moves its arm.

THE BEE-BOTHERED CONDUCTOR
Our conductor is trying to swat a bee with his baton, much to the confusion of the musicians!

CHARLOTTE THE CELLIST
Charlotte plays her cello
by moving the bow in her
left hand.

GUY THE GUITARIST
Guy plays the guitar
by strumming it with his
right hand.

DENISE THE DRUMMER
Denise beats on the
drums as her felt arms
flap up and down.

How to make the conductor

To make the conductor you will need a long, sharpened pencil or balsa wood stick for the support, a thinner stick, a cotton ball or ping-pong ball for the head, yarn for the hair, a plasticine nose, felt, a drawing pin, white cardboard and a felt-tip pen.

1

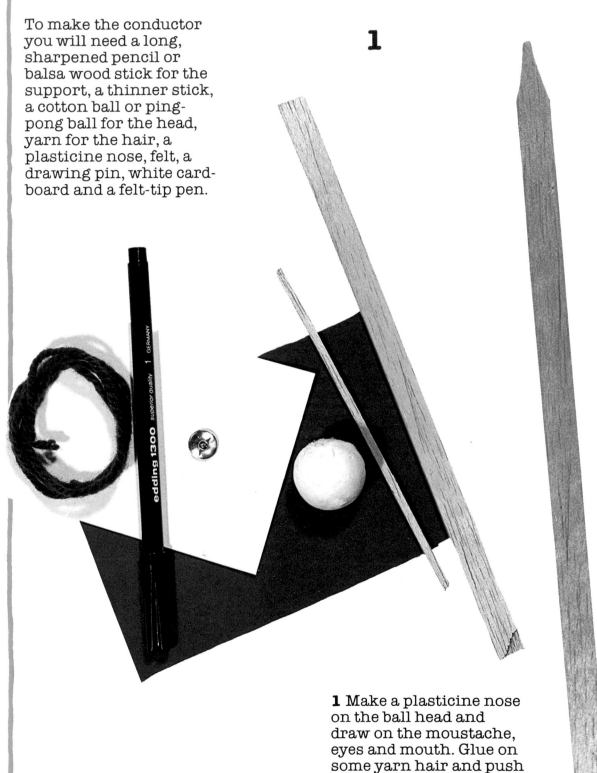

1 Make a plasticine nose on the ball head and draw on the moustache, eyes and mouth. Glue on some yarn hair and push a pointed stick into the head.

2 Cut out felt for the jacket (**A**) and a white cardboard shirt front (**B**). Cut two pieces of felt (**C**) and roll them (**D**) to make the legs.

2

A

B

C

D

3 Glue the legs to the stick and wrap the cape around, over the shirt front, as shown.

3

4 Cut felt for the arms and glue them to the body. Glue the stick and baton to one hand.

4

Marionettes

Marionettes are string puppets that are worked from above. Like many other kinds of puppets, marionettes have been used to entertain people all over the world for hundreds of years. Here are some simple examples for you to make to add to your puppet show.

You will need dowels or balsa wood sticks, string, ping-pong balls or cotton balls, colored felt, strong glue, plasticine, cardboard and felt-tip pens to decorate.

THE FUNKY CHICKEN

HOW MARIONETTES WORK

To operate a marionette you tilt the crosspiece in various directions so that the puppet walks, dances, pecks or flies. The more strings the puppet has, the more complicated it is to control, so practice in front of a mirror before you give your performance.

THE CONTENTED COW

The crosspiece controlling the cow is strung in a different way from the others so that the cow can move its four legs.

THE FLYING DUCK

The duck is very simple to make. It's made in just three pieces, with a body and two wings. The body has plasticine stuck to it at the bottom to weigh it down. One string is attached to the body and two other strings to the wings. Move the crosspiece up and down and the duck flaps its wings.

How to make the chicken

The funky chicken is made from colored felt, yarn, two sticks, two ping-pong balls or cotton balls, plasticine, string, a paper fastener, glue, cardboard and pens to decorate.

1 Use plasticine for the feet, beak and eyes, yarn for the neck and legs, felt for the comb and put together as shown.

2 Wrap a piece of yellow felt around the other cotton ball for the body. Glue on felt wings and a cardboard collar and tie.

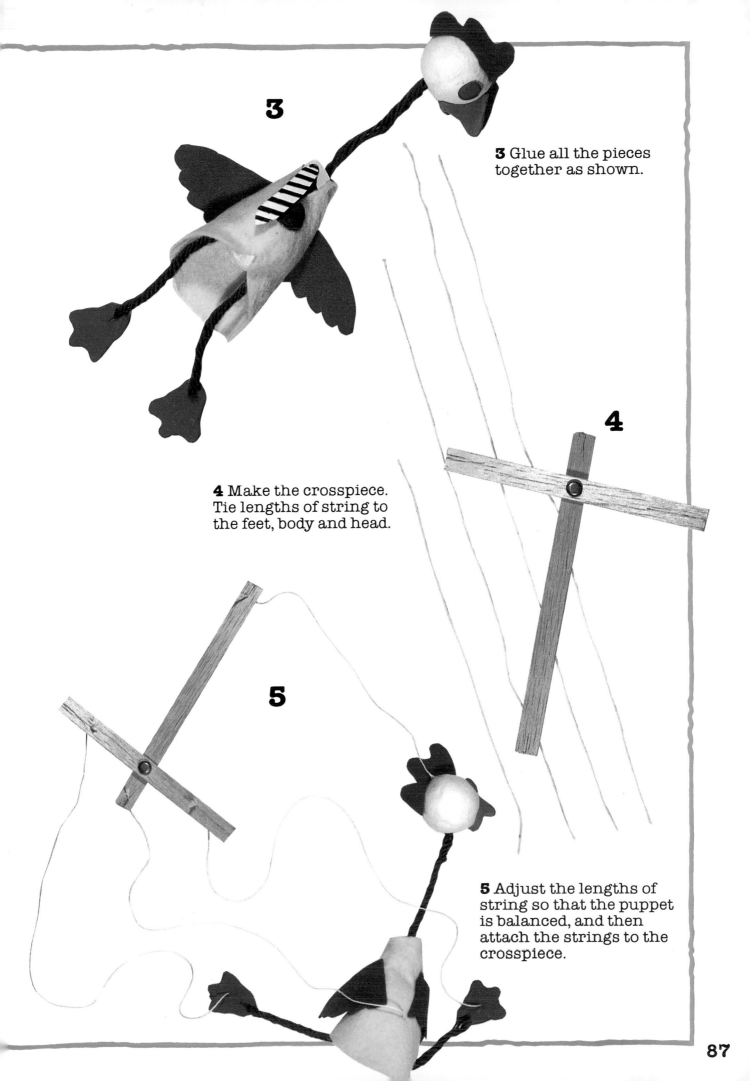

3

3 Glue all the pieces together as shown.

4

4 Make the crosspiece. Tie lengths of string to the feet, body and head.

5

5 Adjust the lengths of string so that the puppet is balanced, and then attach the strings to the crosspiece.

Hand shadows

Hand shadows are another kind of theater. They can be as simple or as complicated as you want to make them. The shadow creatures on the next few pages are quite easy to create, but with a little practice they can be made to act out dramas. Change the position of your fingers and they open and close their eyes. Experiment with different sound effects and move their mouths so that they appear to bark, neigh or screech. They can grow larger and smaller, chase each other or even fight to the death!

To create hand shadows you need a light source behind you and a plain wall in front. You could use a reading lamp, a flashlight or even sunlight. If you don't have a plain white wall, perhaps you could ask a grown-up to pin up a white sheet instead.

RABBIT

DOG

OSTRICH

Hand shadows

ELEPHANT

BIRD

PUNK ROCKER

BABY RABBIT

VULTURE

WOLF

Hand shadows with props

You can create a whole host of exciting hand shadows by using cut-out cardboard props. Quite simple shapes can prove very effective, like the rooster's comb below, or you can make more intricate cut-outs, like the knights doing battle on page 95. For these more complicated shadows, make sure you use a strong light source and have your hands quite close to the wall. That way the shadow will be as clear as possible and you will be able to see all the detail.

ROOSTER
This simple cardboard cut-out is the rooster's comb. Glue or tape a loop of cardboard to its base for your finger. You can use your other hand to create the rooster's feathers.

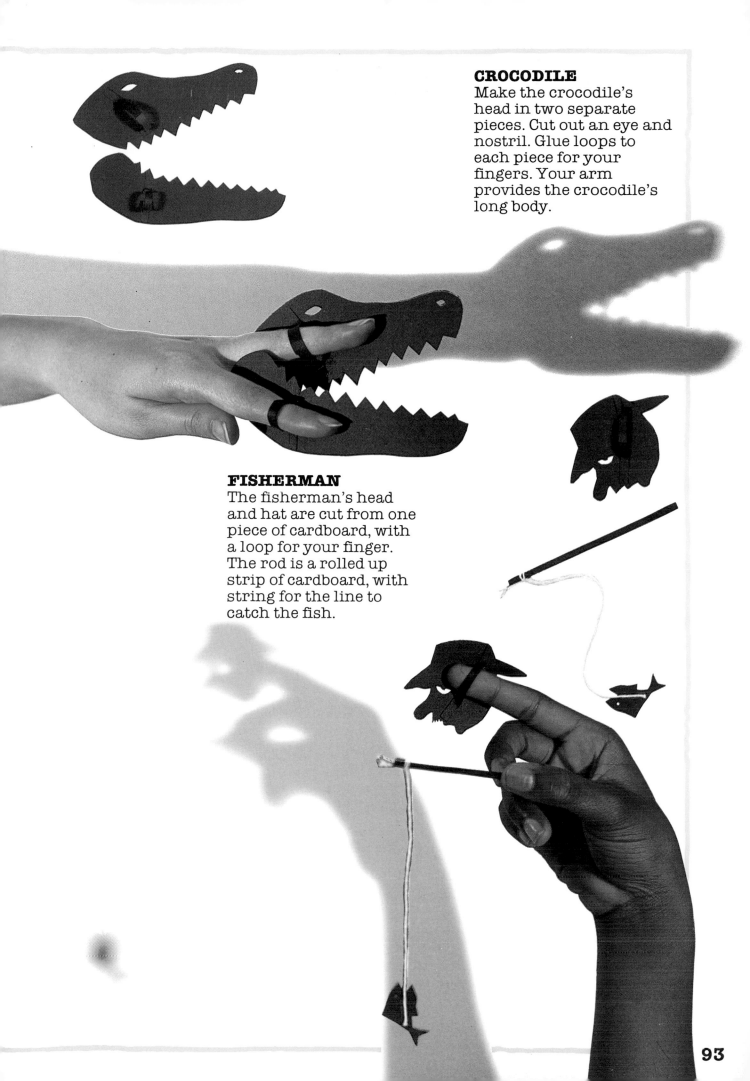

CROCODILE
Make the crocodile's head in two separate pieces. Cut out an eye and nostril. Glue loops to each piece for your fingers. Your arm provides the crocodile's long body.

FISHERMAN
The fisherman's head and hat are cut from one piece of cardboard, with a loop for your finger. The rod is a rolled up strip of cardboard, with string for the line to catch the fish.

Hand shadows with props

THE BOXERS
These mean-looking boxers are all ready to fight it out. Cut out their heads and boxing gloves and attach loops. Put them on your fingers as shown and let the match begin!

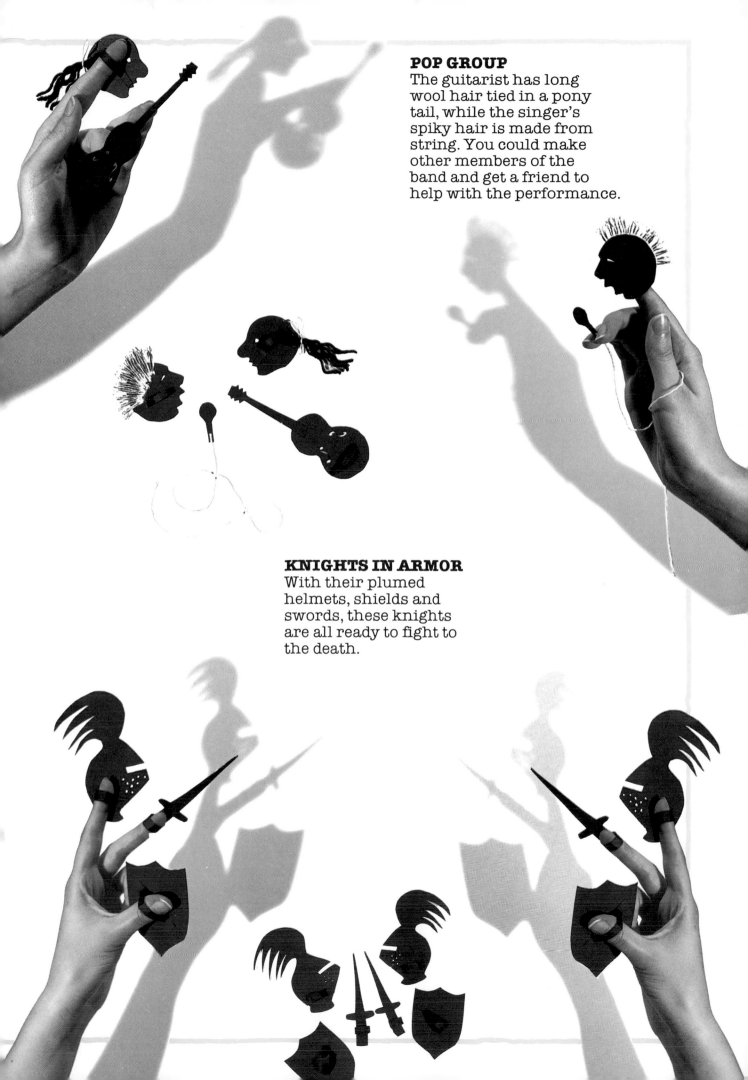

POP GROUP
The guitarist has long wool hair tied in a pony tail, while the singer's spiky hair is made from string. You could make other members of the band and get a friend to help with the performance.

KNIGHTS IN ARMOR
With their plumed helmets, shields and swords, these knights are all ready to fight to the death.

Making a theater

A shadow theater has a translucent screen, which means it lets light shine through. Puppets perform behind the screen so that only the shadow of the figure is seen by the audience. You can make a shadow theater in many different ways. It could be a picture frame with a piece of old sheet stretched across it, or you could cut up a cardboard box, decorate it and tape tracing or wax paper to it.

Our shadow theater below is very simple to make. Cut a circle out of black cardboard, color some appropriate scenery onto tracing paper and glue this to the cardboard. Tie or tape it to a chair and set up the light source.

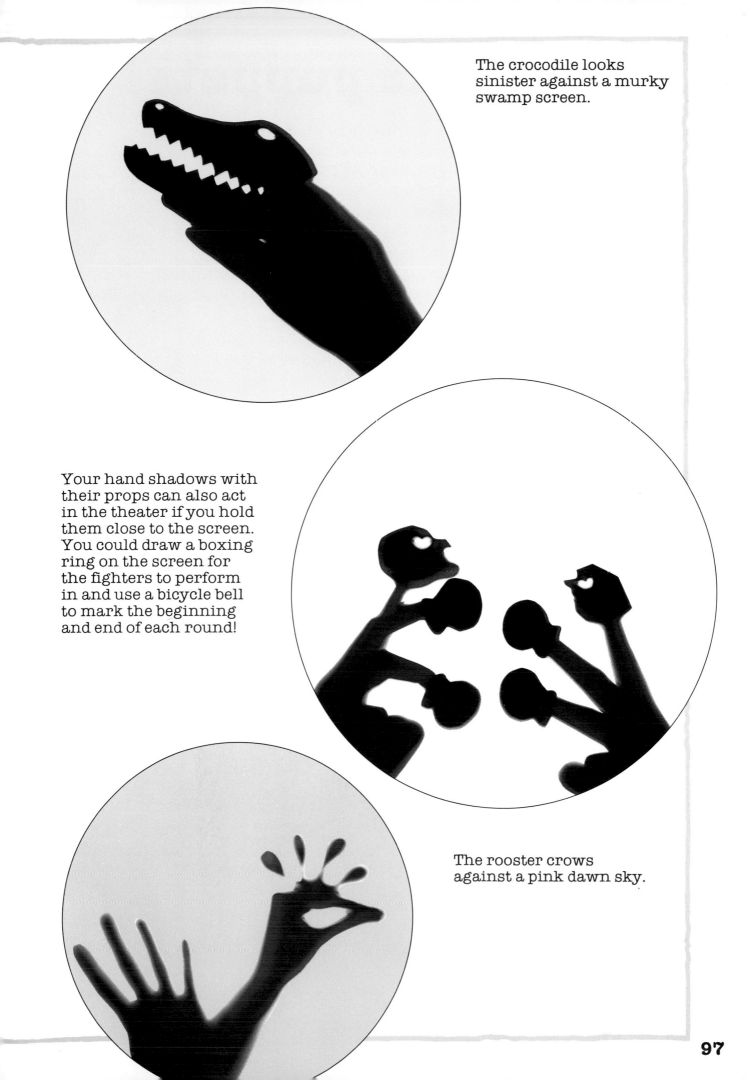

The crocodile looks sinister against a murky swamp screen.

Your hand shadows with their props can also act in the theater if you hold them close to the screen. You could draw a boxing ring on the screen for the fighters to perform in and use a bicycle bell to mark the beginning and end of each round!

The rooster crows against a pink dawn sky.

Simple puppets

Shadow puppets are flat figures, worked by sticks or strings, that you hold against the screen. Traditional shadow puppets were made out of painted and oiled leather or parchment, but you can make excellent shadow puppets out of thin, stiff cardboard.

It's a good idea to make lots of different puppets for your plays. The figures don't all have to look realistic — you can create scary monsters or creatures with one animal's head and another's body. Use your imagination to make them as funny, fierce, ridiculous or as beautiful as you like.

DINOSAUR
This rather fierce-looking stegosaurus is controlled by a stick glued to its back.

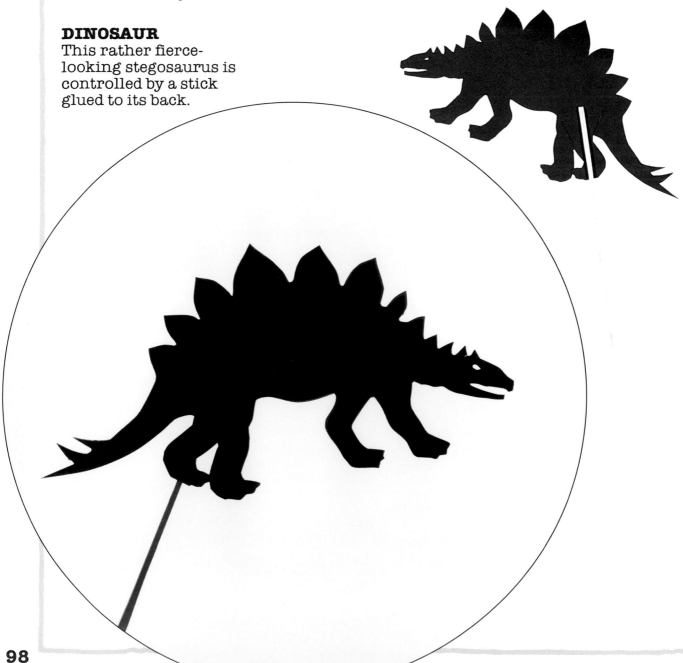

SPIDER
This big spooky spider with its sharp fangs showing is hanging by a thread behind the screen.

MONKEY
Paint your screen to look like a jungle and let the monkey swing through the trees by the thread tied to his tail.

Paper airplane

There are many toys you can make yourself and paper airplanes are probably the quickest. Yet they can be spectacular flying craft, accurate and fast. There are endless designs for paper airplanes and many simply involve the careful folding of a single sheet of paper. Try experimenting with your own designs. Cut out wings, trim the tail or weight the nose until you have lift off!

1 Take a rectangular sheet of stiff paper and make the first fold as shown. Unfold.

1

2 Take the folded corner across to the opposite side and make the second fold. Unfold.

2

3 Open out the sheet of paper. Fold across the middle point of the two creases.

3

4 Using the creases as your guide, fold in the two sides so that you are left with this triangle shape.

4

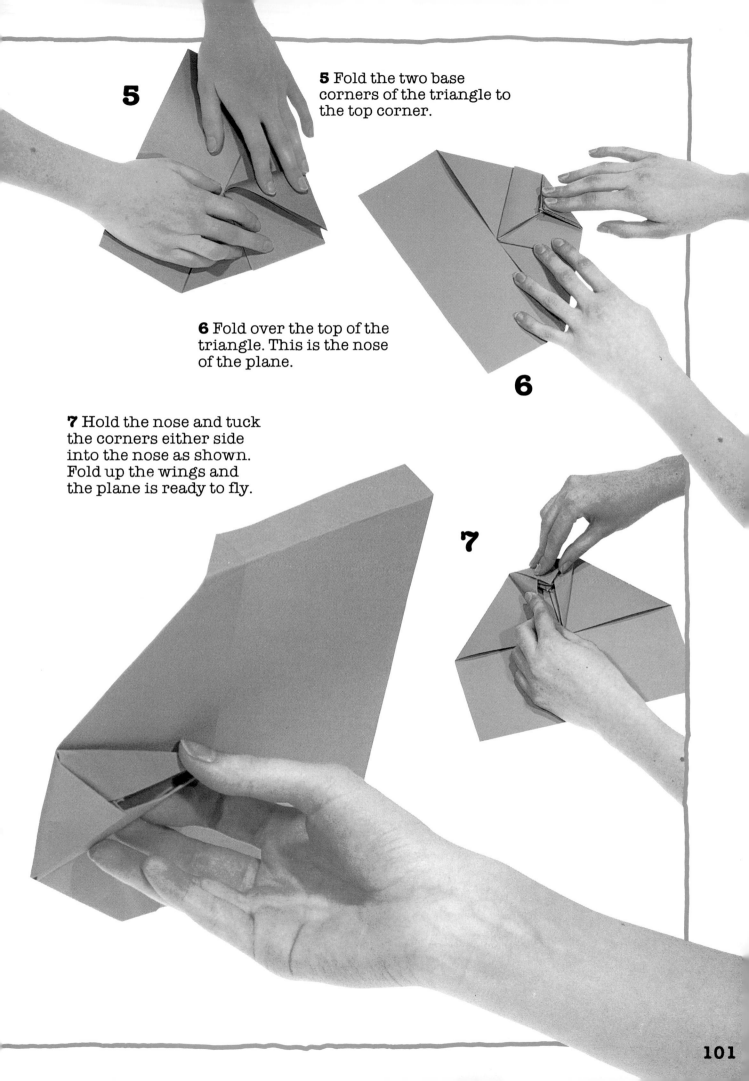

5

5 Fold the two base corners of the triangle to the top corner.

6

6 Fold over the top of the triangle. This is the nose of the plane.

7 Hold the nose and tuck the corners either side into the nose as shown. Fold up the wings and the plane is ready to fly.

7

Balloon rocket

This balloon rocket is great fun. It whizzes along a string at top speed.

You will need a long balloon, drinking straw, tape, bulldog clip, string (at least nine feet), cardboard, colored pencils, and scissors.

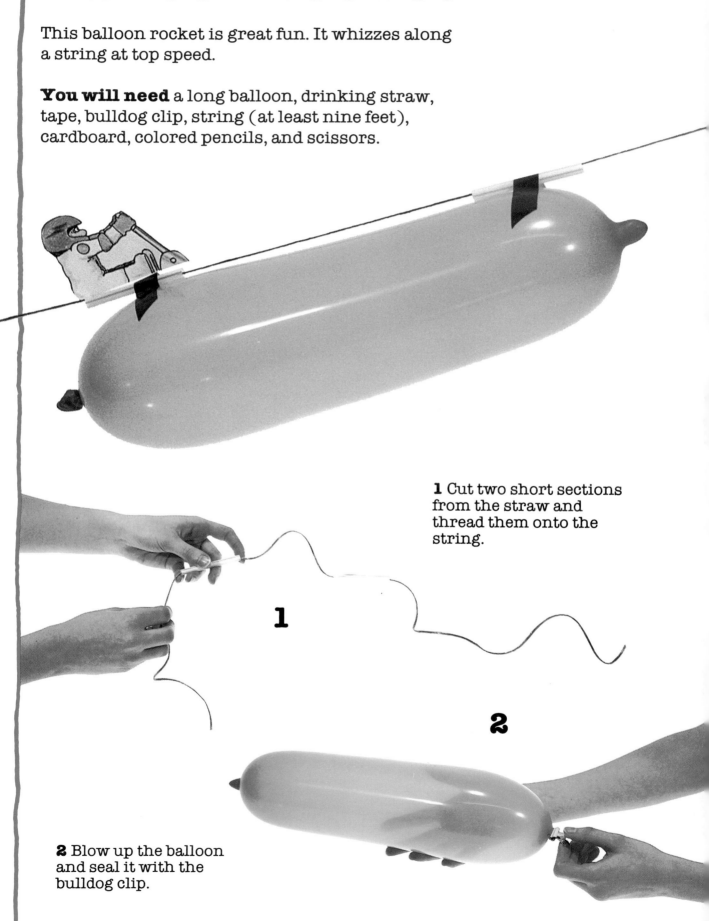

1 Cut two short sections from the straw and thread them onto the string.

2 Blow up the balloon and seal it with the bulldog clip.

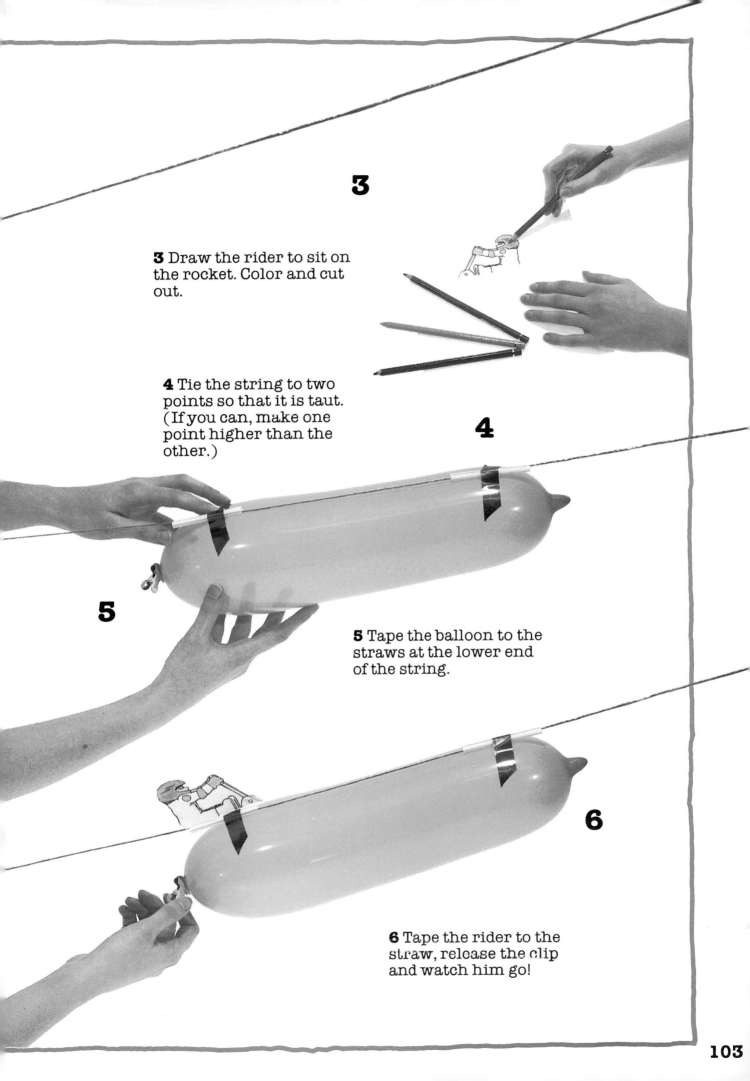

3

3 Draw the rider to sit on the rocket. Color and cut out.

4 Tie the string to two points so that it is taut. (If you can, make one point higher than the other.)

4

5

5 Tape the balloon to the straws at the lower end of the string.

6

6 Tape the rider to the straw, release the clip and watch him go!

Parachute

This brightly colored parachute is actually made from a trash can liner!

You will need a trash can liner, colored tape, string, a small toy, and scissors.

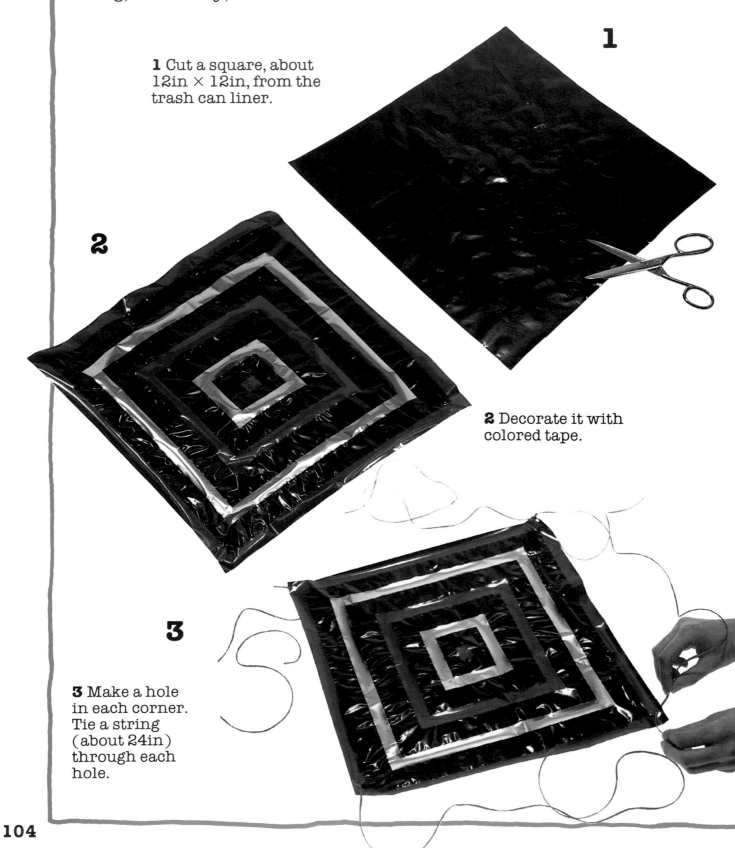

1 Cut a square, about 12in × 12in, from the trash can liner.

2 Decorate it with colored tape.

3 Make a hole in each corner. Tie a string (about 24in) through each hole.

4 Tie the four strings to a
small toy. You may have
to experiment with toys
of different weights.

4

THE LAUNCH
To launch the parachute,
fold it up and throw it
high into the air.

Frisbee

Frisbee throwing is a great game. Once you've mastered the technique, you'll be surprised at how far the frisbee can travel.

You will need four paper plates, scissors, gummed shapes, glue, paint, and a paintbrush.

1 Cut out the centers from four paper plates.

1

2

2 Decorate two of the rings. We have used bright paint and gummed dots.

3 Glue the four rings together so that the decorated rings are top and bottom.

3

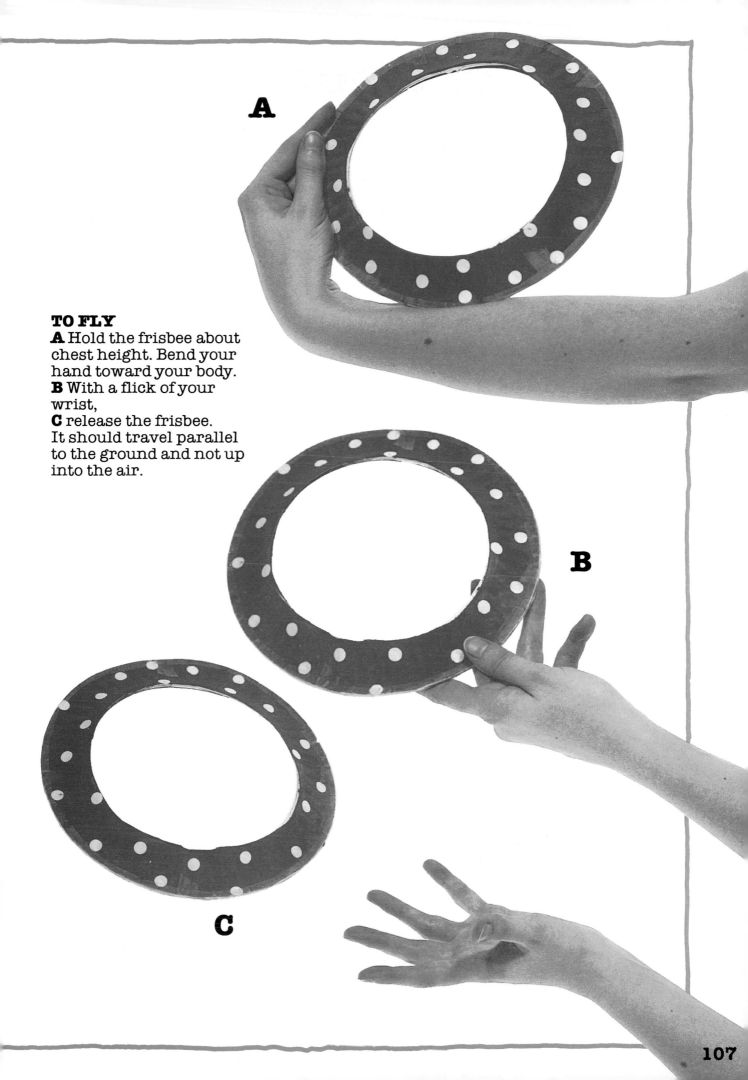

A

TO FLY
A Hold the frisbee about chest height. Bend your hand toward your body.
B With a flick of your wrist,
C release the frisbee. It should travel parallel to the ground and not up into the air.

B

C

Traditional kite

Kite flying was probably invented in China, more than 2,000 years ago. This simple kite will fly in the slightest of winds.

You will need a plastic bag, 2 light garden stakes, string, strong tape, kite cord and spindle, paints and paintbrush.

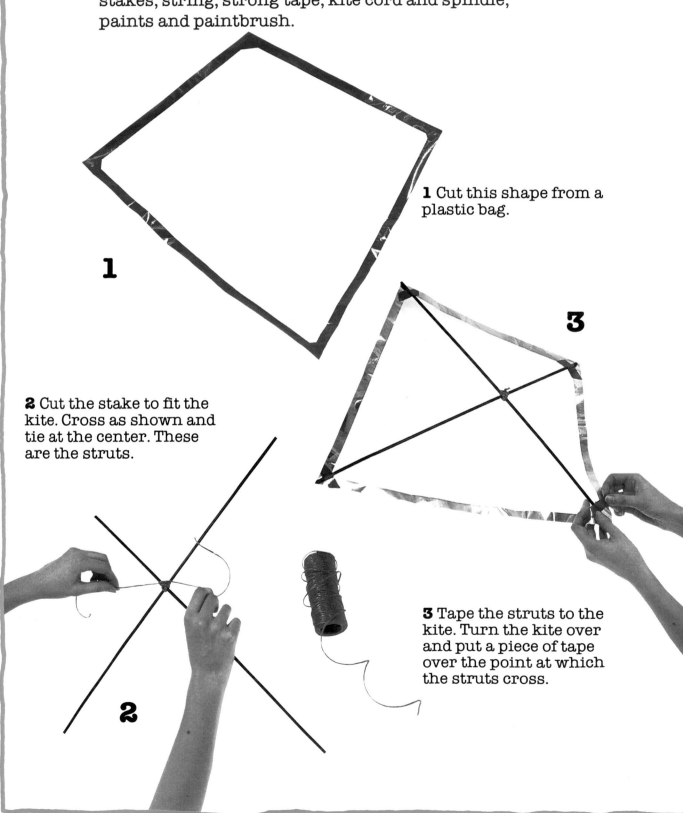

1 Cut this shape from a plastic bag.

2 Cut the stake to fit the kite. Cross as shown and tie at the center. These are the struts.

3 Tape the struts to the kite. Turn the kite over and put a piece of tape over the point at which the struts cross.

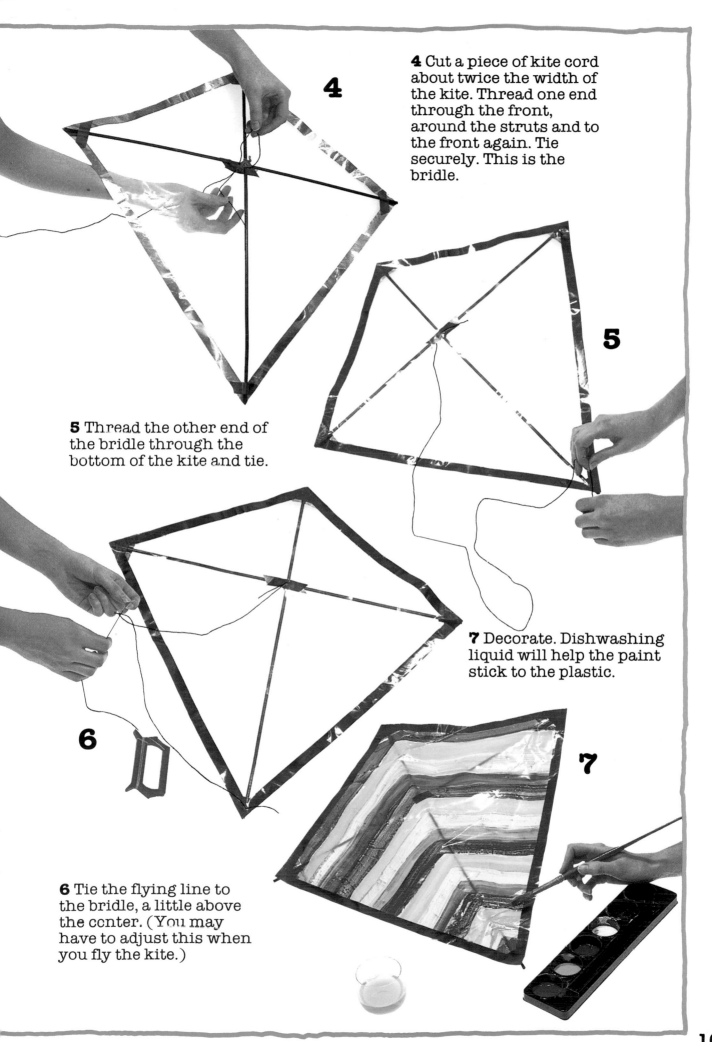

4 Cut a piece of kite cord about twice the width of the kite. Thread one end through the front, around the struts and to the front again. Tie securely. This is the bridle.

5 Thread the other end of the bridle through the bottom of the kite and tie.

7 Decorate. Dishwashing liquid will help the paint stick to the plastic.

6 Tie the flying line to the bridle, a little above the center. (You may have to adjust this when you fly the kite.)

Kite flying

The bridle
Read the advice on page 126 before you start. The short strings from the kite to the flying line are called the bridle. They hold the kite at the correct angle to the wind.

HOW TO FLY A KITE

To launch the kite, unwind about 60 feet of line. Get a friend to hold the kite above his head, with the tail behind him.

When the kite is up in the air, pull down on the line to get more height. Work the line so that the kite leans forward into the wind.

As he releases the kite, you walk backward until the kite begins to rise. Then gradually let out more line.

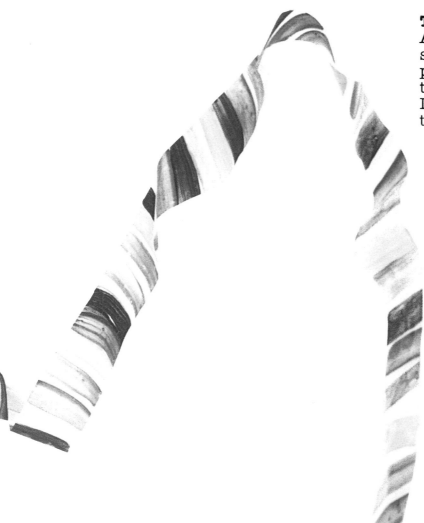

The tail

A tail gives the kite stability. Make it out of plastic (about five times the height of the kite). Decorate and tape it to the bottom of the kite.

Clown kite

This clown kite doesn't need a tail. The hole in its mouth gives it the stability it needs. The shape is important, so turn to page 126 for the proportions.

You will need plastic, strong tape, garden stakes, kite cord and spindle, scissors, paints, and paintbrush.

1 Cut out the shape of the kite according to the proportions on page 126. Tape the edges.

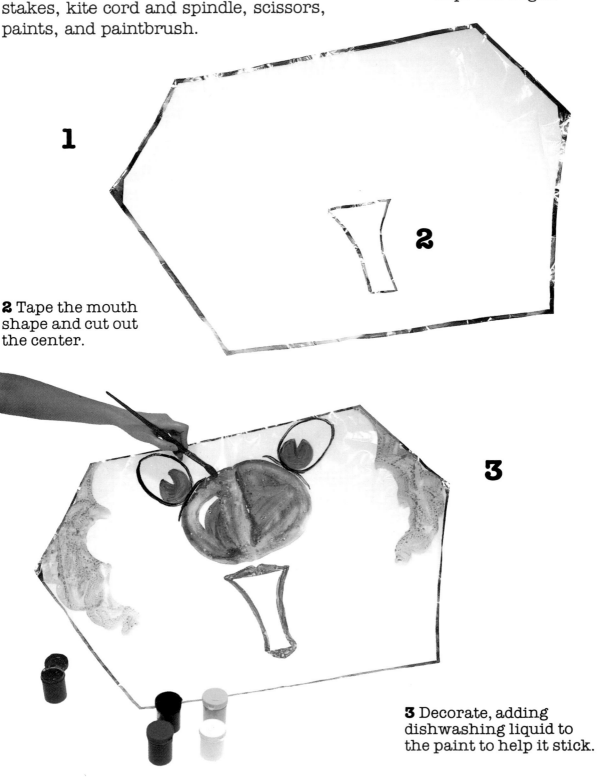

1

2

2 Tape the mouth shape and cut out the center.

3

3 Decorate, adding dishwashing liquid to the paint to help it stick.

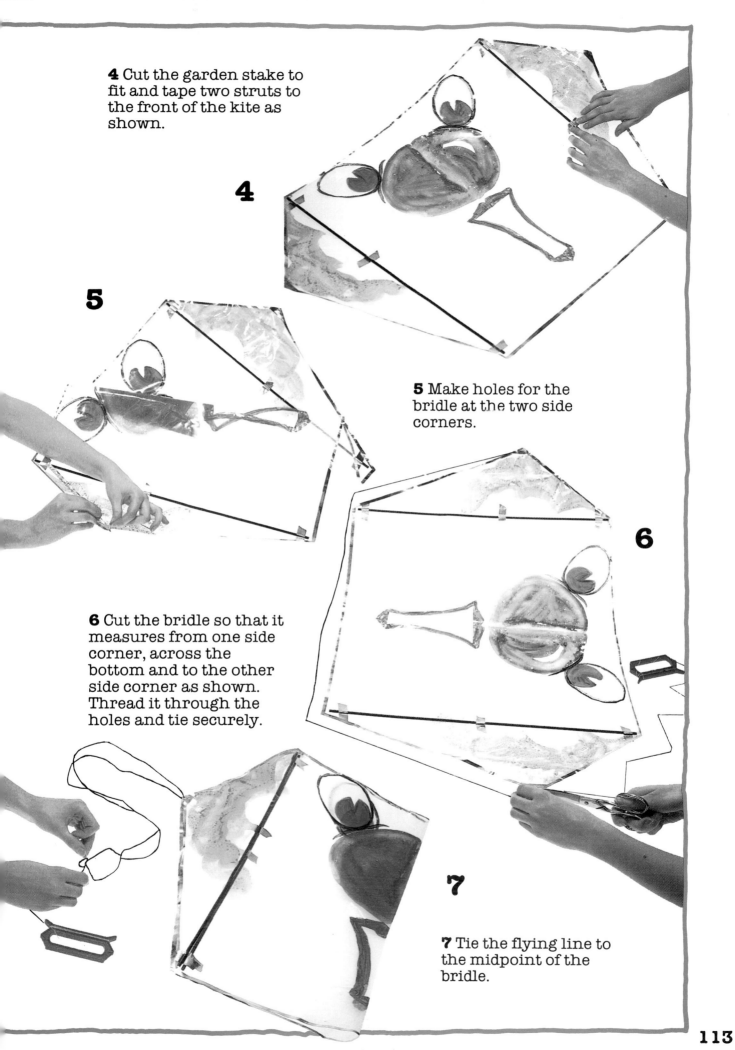

4 Cut the garden stake to fit and tape two struts to the front of the kite as shown.

4

5

5 Make holes for the bridle at the two side corners.

6

6 Cut the bridle so that it measures from one side corner, across the bottom and to the other side corner as shown. Thread it through the holes and tie securely.

7

7 Tie the flying line to the midpoint of the bridle.

Flying the clown

You may have to experiment to see which of
your kites fly best in different kinds of weather.
This clown kite will fly well in either a strong or
a light wind. See advice on page 126.

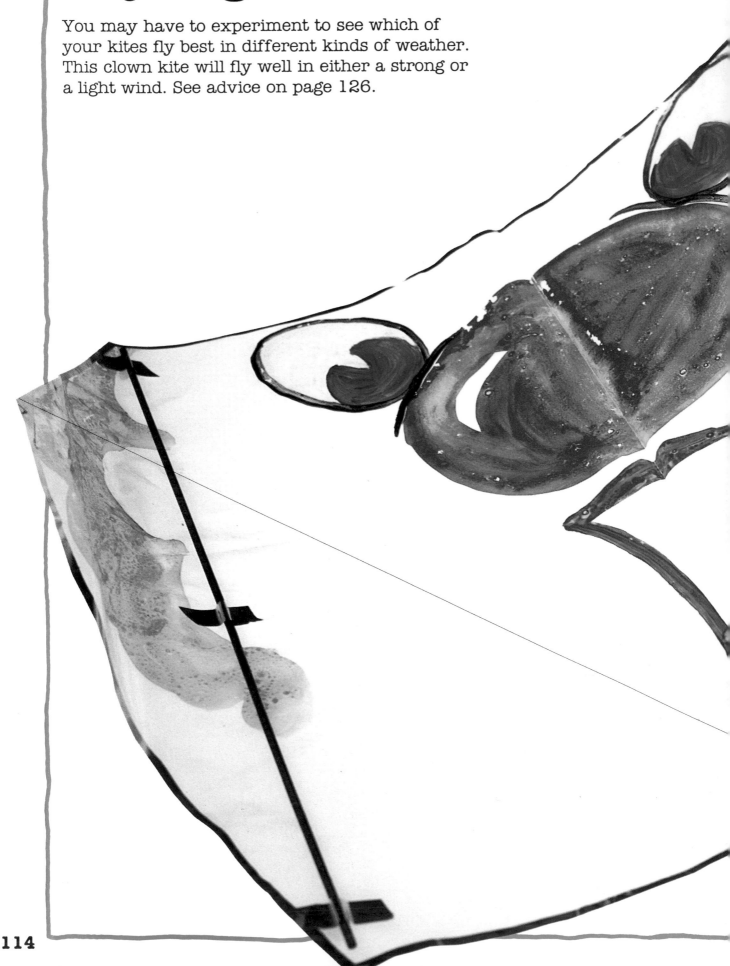

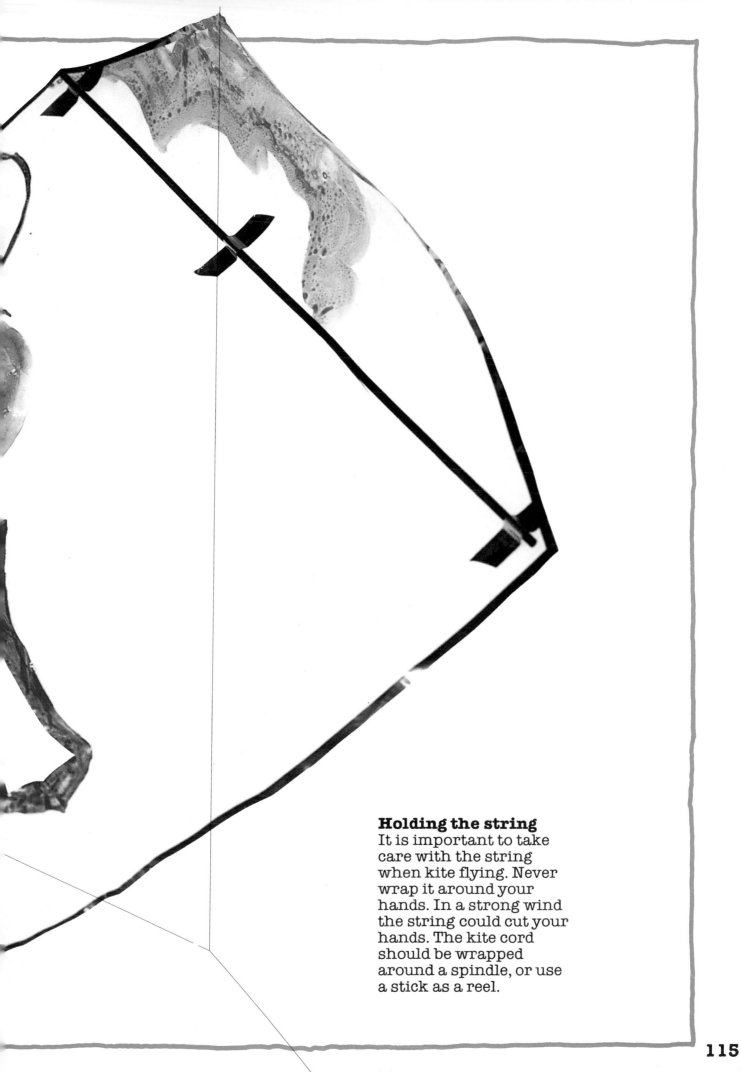

Holding the string
It is important to take care with the string when kite flying. Never wrap it around your hands. In a strong wind the string could cut your hands. The kite cord should be wrapped around a spindle, or use a stick as a reel.

Eggshells, eggcups, cress
seeds, cotton and felt-tip
pens to decorate.

"Instant" plants

Growing plants can be an indoor activity. Some
seeds grow very quickly under the right conditions.
Mustard and cress plants don't need soil and they
take only about two weeks until they are ready to
be cut. You could grow the plants in funny eggshell
faces, or you could sprinkle some seeds on a tray in
the shape of a letter or number and then watch the
plants magically spell out your initial or age.

Green-thumb tips
Cress seeds grow more slowly than mustard so
if you want to grow them to eat together, sow
cress four days before the mustard. Mustard is
also very peppery, so sow more cress than
mustard.

1

1 Carefully clean out an
empty eggshell and then
decorate it with a face.
Use your imagination
and make it funny or
fierce, surprised or
angry, a human, an
animal or even a
monster!

2

2 Put some damp cotton into the eggshell head and sprinkle the cress seeds on top.

3

3 Put the eggshell in a warm dark place. Do not let the cotton dry out. Spray regularly to keep the seeds damp.

4 When the plants are about 5 in high, put them in the light. About two weeks after sowing the seeds, your funny faces will have sprouted green hair!

4

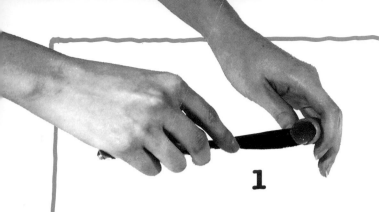

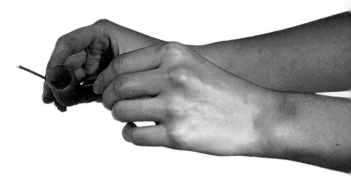

1 Try growing an upside
down carrot plant and
compare it with one you
grow on a saucer. Cut the
carrot to about 2 in and
trim the leaves. Carefully
hollow out the top.

2 Push a strong
toothpick or small twig
through the scooped out
carrot.

Vegetable toppers

Fresh vegetable tops can be used to grow pretty
and unusual plants. Beet tops grow veined
reddish-green leaves and carrot tops grow into
ferns. Parsnips, turnips, radishes and even
pineapples (if the center has not been cut out)
will all make attractive plants. They will live for
only a few weeks, but they are cheap and easy
plants to grow.

Green-thumb tips

Trim the vegetables to about $1/2$ in from the top
and the leaves to about 1 in. Put them in plates
of water or on saucers of pebbles in water.
Make sure you don't let them dry out. Keep
them in a fairly warm, sunny place. Leaves will
start to grow in about two weeks.

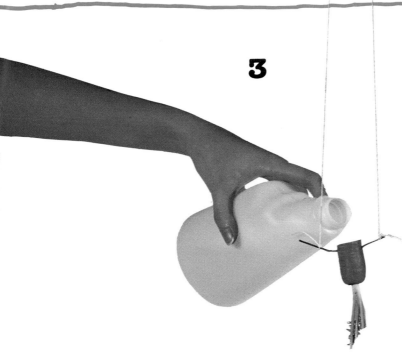

3 Tie a length of string to each end of the twig and hang the carrot up in a warm, sunny place. Fill the carrot with water and refill it regularly. You will find that the leaves will turn and grow upward, making a pretty and unusual plant.

The pineapple, radish and turnip are growing on saucers of pebbles in water.

Try growing lots of different vegetable tops to compare how they grow.

Turnip

Radish

Pineapple

GROWING PUMPKINS
Buy pumpkin seeds from a garden shop. Sow the seeds in pots and then follow the instructions on the packet. Your pumpkin plant will need a lot of attention. Good luck!

Jack-o-lantern

An illuminated pumpkin with a wicked grin is one of the exciting sights of Halloween. Most people buy their pumpkins, but if you like a challenge you could try growing your own. They can grow up to two feet wide, weigh as much as 50 pounds and will take about four months to grow.

Green-thumb tips
The seedling can be raised in a pot, but to produce a good pumpkin you will need a well fertilized garden plot.

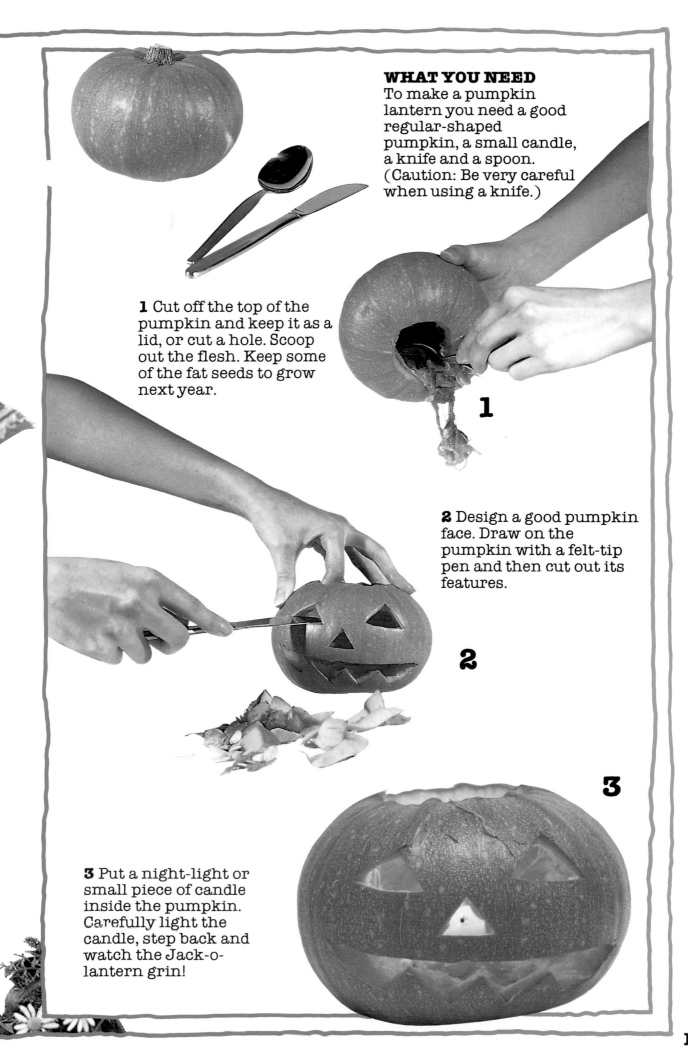

WHAT YOU NEED
To make a pumpkin
lantern you need a good
regular-shaped
pumpkin, a small candle,
a knife and a spoon.
(Caution: Be very careful
when using a knife.)

1 Cut off the top of the
pumpkin and keep it as a
lid, or cut a hole. Scoop
out the flesh. Keep some
of the fat seeds to grow
next year.

1

2 Design a good pumpkin
face. Draw on the
pumpkin with a felt-tip
pen and then cut out its
features.

2

3

3 Put a night-light or
small piece of candle
inside the pumpkin.
Carefully light the
candle, step back and
watch the Jack-o-
lantern grin!

Miniature garden

With a little imagination, you can create a miniature garden out of lots of different things. Small mirrors become ponds, rocks become boulders and strangely-shaped twigs turn into dramatic dead trees. We've used a terra-cotta tray for our garden, but a large plastic bowl would do.

Green-thumb tips

You need slow-growing plants for this garden. Ask in a plant store which they think will be suitable. You could also look around for cuttings, and of course moss and lichen are free. Look for moss on the bark of trees, in grass and in the cracks of paving stones and walls.

WHAT YOU NEED
A shallow tray, a mirror for a pond, stones and pebbles, moss and lichen, slow-growing plants, such as miniature conifers or herbs, and potting soil.

1

1 Put a layer of potting soil in the tray. Position any large stones. Put in your mirror pond, hiding its edges with potting soil. Roughly work out where you want the plants.

2

2 Put in the plants and shrubs. Think about the different colors of the plants and try to arrange them so that you get as much color contrast as possible. Water carefully and if you like, decorate with small figures.

123

Cactus garden

You can have great fun making this desert scene. Cacti are fascinating plants to grow because of their strange shapes and the startlingly bright flowers they occasionally surprise you with. They look most effective when you plant lots of different kinds together. Paint an appropriate picture to stand behind your garden and the desert scene is complete!

Green-thumb tips
Cacti come from hot countries so they like a warm sunny room. They store water in their thick stems and don't need much watering. Water lightly (preferably with rainwater) in spring and summer, but let the soil almost dry out in winter.

WHAT YOU NEED
Different kinds of cacti, (choose some which flower when small, and remember you can also take cacti "cuttings" from friends), a shallow tray, pebbles, gravel, sandy soil, gardening gloves and heavy paper.

1 Put a layer of pebbles in the bottom of the tray for drainage. Cover with the sandy soil.

1 + 2

3

2 Plant your cacti in the way shown, using gardening gloves and a piece of heavy paper to protect your hands.

4

3 Water the soil lightly, cover the spaces between the cacti with gravel and spray again.

4 Use your imagination to paint a desert scene and stand it up behind your cactus garden.

125

WARNING!

Always take care when flying your kites. Never fly your kites near overhead power lines, near a road or railroad, near an airport or in a thunderstorm.

The best place to choose is an open area of parkland away from trees, the windy side of a hill, or at the beach.

Handy hints

Be very careful when using scissors or knives – always ask an adult to help you with difficult cutting procedures.

If a project involves using paint or glue, cover your work surface with newspaper before you begin – and always be prepared to tidy up afterward.

Do not be disappointed if at first your project is not quite perfect – try again.

Look around at home for useful materials and save them for your rainy day.

Items you will need again and again are: crayons, felt-tips, string, colored paper, tracing paper, yarn, cardboard, sticky tape, paper plates, cardboard tubes and boxes, cardboard cartons and plastic bottles (well washed out), ribbon, shells, drinking straws, old socks and rubber gloves, egg cartons, sticky shapes, paintbrushes, paper fasteners, scissors and glue.

If you cannot find all you need to make a project, think again – you will probably find alternative materials that can work just as well.

Have fun!

Clown kite

Use these proportions for the clown kite. It can be made any size you want.

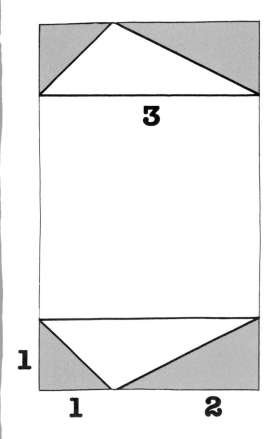

Index

balloon rocket 102-3
bits and pieces 34-5

card tricks 60-71
  abracadabra trick 70-1
  burning building trick
    66-7
  clever cut trick 68-9
  crafty glimpse trick
    64-5
  spot the dot trick 60-1
  suit-able trickery 62-3
  see also magic tricks
cookies 38-41
cooking 36-43
  ginger cookies 38-9
  icing cookies 40-1
  marzipan treats 43
  peppermint creams 42
  salad faces 36-7
Costumes 10-15
  bumblebee 14-15
  skeleton 12-13
  witch 10-11

frisbee 106-7

growing plants 116-25
  cactus garden 124-5
  "instant" plants 116-17
  miniature garden
    122-3
  mustard and cress
    116-17
  pumpkins 120
  vegetable toppers
    118-19

Halloween 11, 12, 120
hand shadows 88-97
  baby rabbit 91
  bird 90
  boxers 94, 97
  crocodile 93, 97
  dog 89
  elephant 90
  fisherman 93
  knights in armor 95
  ostrich 89
  pop group 95

punk rocker 90
rabbit 89
rooster 92, 97
using props 92-5
vulture 91
wolf 91
handy hints 126

Jack-o-lantern 120-1

kites 108-15
  clown kite 112-15
  flying a kite 110-11,
    114-15
  proportions 126
  traditional kite 108-9

magic tricks 44-59
  coin trick 46-7
  educated egg trick 44
  eggs-periment trick 45
  levitation 54-5
  magic cord trick 50-1
  mind reading 52
  Pharaoh's finger trick
    53
  ribbon magic trick
    58-9
  sleight-of-hand 46
  swordbox trick 56-7
  vanishing glass trick
    48-9
  see also card tricks
masks 18-33
  Cyclops mask 21
  eagle mask 22-3
  elephant mask 33
  frog mask 25
  mouse mask 32
  paper bag masks
    22-5
  paper plate masks 18-
    21
  papier mâché masks
    30-3
  robot mask 26-9
  rooster mask 24
  sunflower mask 20
  three-dimensional
    masks 26-7

paper airplane 100-1
paper plate masks 18-21
papier mâché masks 30,
  32-3
parachute 104-5
party hats 6-9
  King of the Castle 7
  Neptune's Crown 8
  Queen of Hearts 6
  Woodland Crown 9
pirate 35
placemats 16-17
puppets 72-87
  Angry Andy 77
  bee-bothered conductor
    80, 82-3
  Charlotte the Cellist 81
  contented cow 85
  Dancing Dandy 72-3
  Denise the Drummer
    81
  dinosaur 98
  Fiona Fairflax 77,
    78-9
  flying duck 85
  funky chicken 84,
    86-7
  glove puppets 76-9
  Guy the Guitarist 81
  Kevin the Clown 77
  marionettes 84-7
  monkey 99
  Patricia Panda 76
  puppet toys 72-5
  shadow puppets 98-9
  spider 99
  stick puppets 80-3
  swinging monkey
    74-5

salad faces 36-7
  fruity face 37
  green man 37
shadow theater 88-96,
  98-9
  hand shadows 88-96
  shadow puppets 98-9

tricks *see* card tricks
  and magic tricks